BREAKING
GENERATIONAL
CURSES

BREAKING GENERATIONAL CURSES

OVERCOMING THE LEGACY
OF SIN IN YOUR FAMILY

by

Marilyn Hickey

Harrison House
Tulsa, Oklahoma

18 17 16 15 14   22 21 20 19

Breaking Generational Curses—
Overcoming the Legacy of Sin in Your Family
ISBN 13: 978-1-57794-423-2
ISBN 10: 1-57794-423-2
Copyright © 2000 by Marilyn Hickey
Marilyn Hickey Ministries
P.O. Box 17340
Denver, Colorado 80217

Published by Harrison House Publishers
P.O. Box 35035
Tulsa, Oklahoma 74153

TABLE OF CONTENTS

INTRODUCTION

Robert was destined for failure. His father, notorious for prostituting women, committed suicide when Robert was the tender age of eight. When he was fourteen, Robert started his very own street gang that was known for its vicious crimes of violence and hate. At age sixteen, Robert was sentenced to two years in prison for three drive-by shootings and armed robberies. The day before he left for prison, his mother was murdered by a rival street gang seeking revenge. His stepfather was gunned down by the same gang three-and-a-half months later.

I'm sure if we examined Robert's family tree, we would discover generations of his family that either became caught up in a cycle of destructive behavior or, like Robert, were born into it. The good news is that by age twenty, Robert heard the life-changing Word of the Gospel and broke this pattern of behavior by accepting Christ as his personal Lord and Savior. The bad news is that there are many traits in our families—illnesses, attitudes, behavioral characteristics—that are passed down from generation to generation and few people know how to change this destructive trend.

God wants to shed light on the hidden causes of defeat in our families and root out stubborn and seeming impasses. As we discover the truth of God's Word and apply it to our personal lives, we will establish a tradition of blessing for our present and future generations—a life of abundance, fulfillment, and victory in Christ—for our children, our children's children, and the next generation.

There are two sides of the same coin:

I the Lord thy God am a jealous God, visiting the iniquity of the fathers upon the children unto the third and fourth generation of them that hate me.

Exodus 20:5

and:

Know therefore that the Lord thy God, he is God, the faithful God, which keepeth covenant and mercy with them that love him and keep his commandments to a thousand generations.

Deuteronomy 7:9

Do you want to be blessed? Do you want your children to be blessed? Nothing touches you more than your children. When you give place to God in your life, you open yourself to His blessing. But if you give place to the devil—or if you are under a "generational curse"—you are asking for your children to enter into the same curse, and the devil will devour them!

The following story of two American families illustrates the power of generational curses.

Max Jukes was an atheist who married a godless woman. Some 560 descendants were traced:

Three hundred ten died as paupers—150 became criminals, 7 of them murderers—100 were known to be drunkards—and more than half of the women were prostitutes.

The descendants of Max Jukes cost the United States government more than $1.25 million in 19th century dollars.[1]

Jonathan Edwards was a contemporary of Max Jukes. He was a committed Christian who gave God first place in his life. He married a godly young lady, and some 1,394 descendants were traced:

Two hundred ninety-five graduated from college, of whom 13 became college presidents and 65 became professors. Three were elected as United States senators, 3 as state governors, and others were sent as ministers to foreign countries. Thirty became judges, 100 were lawyers, 1 the dean of an outstanding law school. Seventy-five became officers in the military. One hundred were well-known missionaries, preachers, and prominent authors. Another 80 held some form of public office, of whom 3 were mayors of large cities, 1 was the comptroller of the United States Treasury, and another was vice president of the United States.[2]

THE POWER OF GENERATIONAL CURSES

A Cursed Family

Max Jukes
(atheist)

Wife
(godless woman)

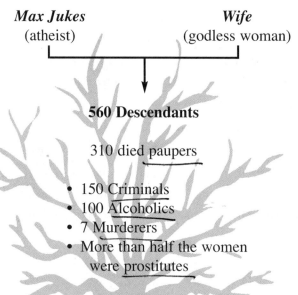

560 Descendants

310 died paupers

- 150 Criminals
- 100 Alcoholics
- 7 Murderers
- More than half the women were prostitutes

Descendants of Max Jukes cost the U.S. government more than $1.25 million in 19th century dollars.

Chart 7

THE POWER OF GENERATIONAL CURSES

A Godly Family

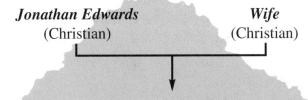

Jonathan Edwards   **Wife**
(Christian)   (Christian)

1394 Descendants

294 College graduates

- 13 College presidents
- 30 Judges
- 1 Dean of a law school
- 80 held public office

- 65 College professors
- 75 Officers in the military
- 100 Well-known missionaries
- 100 Lawyers

- 3 U.S. Senators
- 3 State Governors
- 3 Mayors of large cities
- 1 Comptroller of the U.S. Treasury
- 1 Vice-president of the United States

Not one descendant was a liability to the government.

Chart 8

Not one of the descendants of the Edwards family was a liability to the government!

If you follow God—serving Him, praying, living in the Word, staying committed to Him—then your children and your grandchildren are going to grow up serving Him as well:

Behold, I set before you this day a blessing and a curse; a blessing, if ye obey the commandments of the Lord your God, which I command you this day: and a curse, if ye will not obey the commandments of the Lord your God.

Deuteronomy 11:26-28

And it shall come to pass, if thou shalt hearken diligently unto the voice of the Lord thy God, to observe and to do all his commandments which I command thee this day, that the Lord thy God will set thee on high above all nations of the earth: and all these blessings shall come on thee, and overtake thee, if thou shalt hearken unto the voice of the Lord thy God.

Deuteronomy 28:1,2

DEFINITION OF A
GENERATIONAL CURSE

Generational Curse (jĕn´ə-rā-shən´al kûrs) n.
An uncleansed iniquity that increases in strength
from one generation to the next, affecting the
members of that family and all who come into
relationship with that family.

Chart 2

TAKE THE TEST!

Are you affected by a *Generational Curse?*
Answer the following questions and see!

Do YOU or ANYONE in your family
(including *PAST GENERATIONS):*

☐ 1. Have a pattern of constant failure?

☐ 2. Have a history of untimely deaths and suicides or a
large number of people who have died prematurely?

☐ 3. Exhibit a high level of anger?

☐ 4. Have a high record of accidents or accidents that are
unusual in nature?

☐ 5. Have a history of abuse such as physical, emotional,
or sexual?

☐ 6. Have a history of chronic illness (repeated colds,
long-term health problems, etc.)?

☐ 7. Have a history of mental illness that may have
progressed through generations?

☐ 8. Exhibit any of these personality behaviors: high-
control, manipulation, addiction, co-dependency,
depression, unforgiveness, or social isolation?

☑ If you answered "yes" to any of the questions above,
you could be under a *Generational Curse!*

Chart 2

SECTION 1

The Origin of the Generational Curse

┌───────┐
│   **1**   │
└───────┘

IN THE BEGINNING

In the beginning, God created the perfect family. He created Adam and Eve and placed them in a utopic setting in the Garden of Eden with a charge to be blessed and live an abundant life:

> **And God blessed them, and God said unto them, Be fruitful, and multiply, and replenish the earth, and subdue it: and have dominion over the fish of the sea, and over the fowl of the air, and over every living thing that moveth upon the earth.... I have given you every herb bearing seed, which is upon the face of all the earth, and every tree...to you it shall be for meat. And to every beast of the earth, and to every fowl of the air, and to every thing that creepeth**

**upon the earth, wherein there is life, I have given
every green herb for meat.**

Genesis 1:28-30

Adam and Eve walked in the fullness of God's provision
until Satan deceived them and they lost their dominion over the
earth. Prior to their fall, their family was blessed. After the fall,
however, the curse of sin, death, and destruction entered, and the
family as God originally created it has not been the same since.

Because of their transgression, Adam and Eve placed
themselves under a curse that not only impacted their family, but
all of the families that have come after them. God pronounced a
curse upon the serpent and the land. Adam was sentenced to a
life of hard labor, and Eve's pain during childbearing was
greatly increased. Adam and Eve went from a place of great
abundance, prosperity, and peace to a place of death, disease,
and fear. Every undesirable, hereditary trait which seems to "run
in the family" came directly from the sin of Adam and Eve.
They are directly responsible for what is known today as the
"generational curse."

**To the woman he said, "I will greatly increase
your pains in childbearing; with pain you will give
birth to children"... To Adam he said..."Cursed is the
ground because of you; through painful toil you will
eat of it all the days of your life. It will produce
thorns and thistles for you, and you will eat the**

**plants of the field. By the sweat of your brow you
will eat your food."**

Genesis 3:16-18 NIV

If there is anything that you and I want, it is for our families
to be strong, healthy, and blessed. Yet, from the beginning, we
see the degeneration of the family structure. As we trace Adam
and Eve's family tree, we discover that after they were evicted
from the Garden, Eve gave birth to two sons, Cain and Abel.
Cain became jealous of his brother, Abel, and murdered him.
(Gen. 4:5,8.) Cain's descendant, Lamech, followed in his
forefather's footsteps and also murdered a man. (Gen. 4:23.)
There is a definite hereditary trait that passed from one
generation to the other.

SINS REVISITED

In Exodus 20:5 we discover a profound truth having to do
with these hereditary traits or family weaknesses that are passed
from generation to generation:

Thou shalt not bow down thyself to them [idols]**,
nor serve them: for I the Lord thy God am a jealous
God,** *visiting the iniquity of the fathers* **upon the
children unto the third and fourth generation of
them that hate me.**

I'm sure all of us can think of certain families who have
been ripped apart by such problems as alcoholism, obesity, or
teenage pregnancy. You may be able to examine your own

family tree and recognize a pattern of disease or infirmity. Or you may see a certain characteristic, such as adultery or child abuse, and think, "Wow, my family tree is a mess." Don't panic! God has made a provision for you and your future generations.

Isaiah 53:12 says that Jesus bore our sins. The Bible makes a distinction between the terms *sin, iniquity,* and *transgression.* Not only did Jesus bear our sins on Calvary, but He also bore our transgressions and iniquities:

> **He was wounded for our transgressions, he was bruised for our iniquities: the chastisement of our peace was upon him; and with his stripes we are healed.**
>
> **Isaiah 53:5**

Sin means to miss the mark.[1] So when you sin, you miss the mark or fall below the mark of what God has called you to do. We all have been guilty of missing the mark at some time in our lives: "For all have sinned, and come short of the glory of God..." (Rom. 3:23).

Transgress, on the other hand, means to trespass or overstep preestablished boundaries.[2] We can trespass against man and God. If I were to come up to you and purposely step on your foot or violate your "NO TRESPASSING" sign by entering onto your property without permission, I'd be transgressing against you.

But Jesus was wounded for our transgressions. If you look at the body of Christ, you'll see seven times Jesus' blood was shed: He was circumcised at birth; His beard was plucked; a crown of thorns was pressed on His head; His hands, feet and side were pierced; and His back was beaten. Seven is the number of completion, and I believe God is telling us that Jesus has completely provided for every kind of weakness, infirmity and trangression that we could have through the seven wounds He endured. We can truly say Christ's provision is full and complete.

THE MYSTERY OF INIQUITY

The word *iniquity* means to bend or to distort (the heart). It also implies a certain weakness or predisposition toward a certain sin. Isaiah says Christ was "bruised for our iniquities" (53:5).

> *The word iniquity means "to bend" or "to distort (the heart)."*

If you commit a certain sin once and repent of it and never do it again, then that's the end of it. However, your sin becomes an iniquity when you keep committing that same act; it goes from being a sin to an iniquity, something that is practiced over and over again until it becomes spontaneous. Given certain circumstances or the "right" environment, you will "bend" in that direction.

If a sin is repeatedly committed, it becomes an iniquity which can be passed down through the bloodline. When a person continually transgresses the law, iniquity is created in him and that iniquity is passed to his children. The offspring will have a weakness to the same kind of sin. Each generation adds

If the family tree is not cleansed of this iniquity, then each generation becomes worse and will do what their parents, grandparents and great-grandparents did.

to the overall iniquity, further weakening the resistance of the next generation to sin.

Exodus 20:5 speaks very specifically about the iniquities of the forefathers. If the family tree is not cleansed of this iniquity, then each generation becomes worse and will do what their parents, grandparents, and great-grandparents did. The next generation will bend in the same way of the past generations, and it becomes a bond of iniquity or a generational curse in that family.

We have all seen where one or both parents or grandparents were alcoholics and one or more of the offspring became alcoholics too. And to think it all started as a sin with that one person who overindulged; but because he practiced it and did not repent, his drinking became an iniquity. Consequently, that family begins to bend or have a predisposition toward alcoholism.

Let me give you an example. My father had two nervous breakdowns. I didn't know this until later, but my great-grandfather had mental and emotional problems as well. I never thought of that as being an inherited trait or something that I had a predisposition toward.

When I was thirty-six years old, however, I was under tremendous pressure. The devil spoke to me and said, "You are just like your father. You look and act like him. You are going to have a nervous breakdown just like he did."

I foolishly agreed, "Yes, I'm just like my father. I'm going to have a nervous breakdown too." It was at that point that the Lord spoke to me and said, "That's right! You are just like your Father! I'm your Father, and I've never had a nervous breakdown. And neither will you!"

Jesus was bruised for my iniquities! Through the wounds and bruises He endured on the cross, the provision has been made to restore you and your family to that state of blessedness Adam and Eve once enjoyed in the Garden.

The difference between a wound and a bruise is that if you wound yourself, it will eventually scab over and heal. A bruise, however, can stay around for a long time. It may become discolored and can even go so deep as to bruise the bone. An iniquity can be compared to a bruise because it stays around and goes to the bone from generation...to generation...to generation.

The apostle Paul had a revelation of this when he wrote:

For the mystery of iniquity doth already work.

2 Thessalonians 2:7

The "mystery of iniquity" to which Paul is referring is the unseen and mysterious connection between a father's sins and the path of his children. For example, if the father is a liar and a thief, his children are prone to the same behavior, regardless of their training, social, cultural and environmental influences.

Both sin and iniquity are spiritual terms. We don't always grasp the significance of such terms as we would for something relating to the natural. Paul wrote that the things not seen are understood by the things which are made. (Rom. 1:20.) He was referring to the natural universe—creation—when he spoke of the things that are "made." Likewise, the spiritual can be understood by the natural; for example, diabetes as well as cancer can be an inherited disease.

THE LAW OF GENERATION

Everything produces after its own kind. Within every seed there is inherent ability to reproduce itself. Jesus Himself used this law of generation in the Sermon on the Mount when He said:

> **Beware of false prophets, which come to you in sheep's clothing, but inwardly they are ravening wolves. Ye shall know them by their fruits. Do men gather grapes of thorns, or figs of thistles? Even so every good tree bringeth forth good fruit; but a corrupt tree bringeth forth evil fruit.**
>
> **Matthew 7:15-17**

In the natural, we know that if the fruit is malformed or if the tree is not bearing fruit according to its stock, a mutation has taken place. The same is true in the breeding of animals. If the offspring are not true to the breed, the breeders usually "eliminate" from their pool of animals. Mutants are not wanted. They are a corruption of the line of animals being bred.

As illustrated in the creation of the earth in Genesis 1, everything reproduces after its own kind. We acknowledge this

principle in buying a pedigreed animal, but we completely
ignore this principle when we deal with people.

When you go to a medical doctor for a physical examination
or because you have a medical problem, he will usually take a
medical history before he begins his diagnosis and treatment.
What you tell him of your past problems, and the problems your
parents, grandparents, and siblings may have an effect on what
he may look for and what tests he may order. Many diseases are
genetic or inherent in a family line. These disorders may be in
some or all of the offspring or may skip a generation or two and
occur in the grandchildren or great-grandchildren.

Healthy couples who have healthy ancestors almost always
have healthy offspring. This is the law of generation set in motion
in Genesis 1: everything reproduces after its own kind. Genetic
inheritance is a natural counterpart to spiritual inheritance.
Understanding natural laws concerning genetic inheritance gives
us a working model for the principle of spiritual inheritance.
The Bible gives examples of spiritual laws and their workings in
the lives of various characters and their descendants.

Noah was a man who was "perfect in his generations, and
Noah walked with God" (Gen. 6:9). However, although Noah
was considered "perfect," there were still some flaws in his
bloodline. His son Ham was especially affected by the curse of
iniquity. When Noah became drunk in Genesis 10:20-22, he lost
control of Ham. The weakness to sin caused him to give in to
temptation, and the Bible says that Noah was "uncovered" in his
tent. The Hebrew word for "uncovered" is used in Leviticus
many times, primarily in regard to sexual sins involving incest.

It is highly unlikely that it was a simple case of nudity. The curse that Noah pronounced on Canaan was too drastic for such a trivial thing as that. When we regard God's displeasure with homosexuality, we see that He judged this sin very severely.

Scripture bears out that this was indeed the case with Ham. The Amorites were descendants of Canaan, who in turn descended from Ham. They were in the land of Canaan, which is the land that the Israelites were to take by force from the Amorites. These were the people who were worshiping all manner of idols and false gods, and their worship was characterized by gross sexual perversions and orgies.

THE AMORITES' INIQUITY

In Genesis 15 we read that God gave assurance to Abram that he would inherit the land of promise because his descendants would go to a strange land for four hundred years, but after four generations they would return because "...the iniquity of the Amorites is not yet full" (Gen. 15:16).

If you recall in Genesis 13, Abram and his nephew Lot separated, and Lot chose to settle in a plain where the cities of Sodom and Gomorrah were located. The inhabitants of these cities were also Canaanites. Like the Canaanites, they practiced homosexuality, and their cities were ultimately destroyed because of it.

Abraham negotiated with God for Sodom and Gomorrah, but only righteous Lot and his family were spared. Because the rest of the inhabitants were totally corrupt, they were annihilated. At that time, the iniquity of the Sodomites and the Gomorrahites was full:

> **And Abraham drew near** [to God], **and said, Wilt thou also destroy the righteous with the wicked? Peradventure there be fifty righteous within the city: wilt thou also destroy and not spare the place for the fifty righteous that are therein? ...And the Lord said, If I find in Sodom fifty righteous within the city, then I will spare all the place for their sakes....** [And Abraham said] **Peradventure ten shall be found there. And he said, I will not destroy it for ten's sake.**
>
> **Genesis 18:23,24,26,32**

The mystery of iniquity had already come to pass: the sins of the fathers had been passed to the third and fourth generations of the inhabitants of Sodom and Gomorrah By three or four generations of successive and cumulative iniquity, the children were so crooked and perverse that there was no possibility that they would ever walk uprightly before the Lord. By four generations, their spiritual bloodline was completely corrupt and defiled. Their hearts were inclined only to evil. It was in reference to the Canaanites that God said to Israel in Deuteronomy 20:16,17:

> **But of the cities of these people, which the Lord thy God doth give thee for an inheritance, thou shalt save alive nothing that breatheth: but thou shalt utterly destroy them.**

God's command to Israel was to kill everything that was alive—both people and animals—to kill everything that could harbor evil spirits. The New Testament gives evidence that animals can harbor spirits:

> **Then went the devils out of the man, and entered into the swine: and the herd ran violently down a steep place into the lake, and were choked.**
>
> **Luke 8:33**

The iniquity of the Canaanites was so entrenched that they had to be completely eliminated from the face of the earth in order to destroy their bloodline. To allow them to remain would have subjected Israel to the possibility of becoming contaminated with the same iniquity, and that iniquity would no doubt have spread throughout the nation.

Israel, however, did get into serious trouble when they failed to execute God's judgments. Neglecting to eliminate the Canaanites allowed iniquity to multiply, and when the land fell to iniquity, God brought the sword and purified it. Ezekiel 8 and 9 give a vivid picture of God's having to cleanse the bloodline. In Ezekiel 8 we see the charge God had against Israel—idolatry with its attendant deterioration of moral and social disciplines. And in chapter 9, God commanded angels to slay everyone in the city who didn't have the "mark" of God on his or her forehead:

> **Go ye after him through the city, and smite: let not your eye spare, neither have ye pity: slay utterly old and young, both maids, and little children, and**

**women: but come not near any man upon whom is
the mark; and begin at my sanctuary. Then they
began at the ancient men which were before the
house. And he said unto them, Defile the house, and
fill the courts with the slain: go ye forth. And they
went forth, and slew in the city.**

Ezekiel 9:5-7

Ezekiel recoiled in anguish at the slaughter and feared that
none of the Israelites would be left. God's response to him was
that He was doing what was necessary to cleanse the bloodline:

> **Then said he unto me, The iniquity of the house
> of Israel and Judah is exceeding great, and the land
> is full of blood, and the city full of perverseness: for
> they say, The Lord hath forsaken the earth, and the
> Lord seeth not. And as for me also, mine eye shall
> not spare, neither will I have pity, but I will
> recompense their way upon their head.**

Ezekiel 9:9,10

God assured the prophet that all would be well, because in
the end—after the judgments had fallen and only the righteous
remained—the generations who would come from them would
be righteous and serve the Lord. (Ezek. 14:22,23.)

Iniquity, like sin, must be dealt with. People in both the Old
and New Testaments understood this and traced their sins back
to their forefathers. In Daniel 9:16, Daniel talks about the
iniquity of "our fathers." In Psalm 51:5, David said, "Behold, I
was shapen in iniquity; and in sin did my mother conceive

me." It wasn't the sexual act that was sin, because God created the sexual union for people to reproduce and for pleasure within the bonds of marriage. David was actually saying, "I inherited the iniquity of my fathers, and through conception, their weaknesses have been passed down to me."

Have you ever heard the expression, "You're just like your Aunt So-and-so"? Lamentations 5:7 says, "Our fathers have sinned, and are not; and we have borne their iniquities." In other words, Aunt So-and-so may be dead, but you are carrying her iniquity or that same predisposition to sin.

As I mentioned earlier, I've seen certain behavioral characteristics in my family from time to time that I know are inherited from my parents and grandparents. I recognize them as iniquities, but I've come to realize that I don't have to live under a generational curse—and neither do you! Jesus was bruised for our iniquities, thereby making it possible for us and our children to inherit family blessings.

WHAT BRINGS THE CURSE

Most Christians try their best to walk in the light of God's Word, and they often check on themselves to see if they're sinning against God in some way or another. But when you realize that you can come under a curse for which you are not personally responsible but which you have inherited through your ancestors, that's bad news!

God has been instructing me for a long time about blessings and curses. Some time ago, I became concerned about some of the things that have gone on in the lives of people to whom we have ministered. Terrible things were happening—asthma, cancer, obesity, alcoholism, heart conditions—and God began to show me, piece by piece, where these things really came from.

These things that harass and plague us are actually *family or generational curses*—problems that began back with our ancestors and have been carried through our bloodlines until today. What's worse, they won't stop here, but can be passed on to our children and to our children's children!

THE WORLD KNOWS

Even the world is aware of commonalities in bloodlines. When you fill out an insurance form of any kind, ask it usually, "Is there any history of heart disease in your family?" "Diabetes?" "Cancer?" "Mental illness?" Why do they ask that? Because doctors understand that if such problems or diseases are in your background, you could have them too.

The mother of a woman on our staff died of an asthma-like condition. Sure enough, this woman began to suffer the same symptoms which had killed her mother. I believe that an evil spirit of disease had attacked the mother; and then when she died, that spirit waited for the next generation to attack again.

Wally and I have an adopted son, Michael. Mike was three-and-a-half when we adopted him, and he has experienced many different problems through the years. I used to wonder, *We raised him right. Why does he still experience such difficulties?*

Of course, we did some things wrong; there's no question of that, and we repented of the things we did wrong. But I thought, *I never taught him to do these things, so where did they come from?*

Then I began to see that these hideous things come down from generation to generation, attacking one family member after the next. Mike didn't get those problems from Wally or me; he got them from somewhere in his biological family's history. But we're his adopted and spiritual family, and we've taken authority over the problems and have released him from the generational curse!

MY FAMILY HISTORY

I was visiting my eigty-three-year-old aunt in Sewickley, Pennsylvania. She was so healthy and doing so well that I asked her, "What is the longevity of our family?"

My maiden name is Sweitzer, and she answered, "Well, the Sweitzers have a history of heart trouble. Most of them die of heart trouble." She began to tell me about their life spans. She also told me about my maternal grandmother: "Those are the ones who have the real longevity—they do not have heart problems."

I had a heart problem, but I didn't realize that it had come from my father's background. I was healed of that heart condition because I claimed that Jesus Christ came to break the curse for me! So when I heard about my father's history of heart trouble, I began to break that curse over my daughter Sarah's life.

I know that Sarah is not going to have a heart problem. The devil is not going to come and attack Sarah—and Sarah's children and grandchildren aren't going to have heart problems either, because we've stopped the devil in his tracks!

Alcoholism Is Not Necessarily a Sickness

Proverbs 26:2 says, "The curse causeless shall not come." If we see sin and various troubles affecting our family, that sin is always a curse. Sickness is always a part of the curse. Poverty can pass from generation to generation. God's Word tells us that these things don't just come on their own—there is a cause.

Alcohol is one of the devil's favorite tools to open the door to a hideous curse. Many people believe that social drinking is acceptable, but I tell you: *alcoholism is not so much a sickness as it is a sin.* And sin will always bring a curse.

Another woman on our staff told me that her grandfather was an alcoholic; and her father was an alcoholic; and then her brother was an alcoholic. That's a curse, and it comes down through the generations.

When people get drunk, they do things they wouldn't normally do because their will is broken down. Habakkuk 2:15,16 tells us about this:

Woe unto him that giveth his neighbor drink, that puttest thy bottle to him, and makest him drunken also, that thou mayest look on their nakedness! Thou art filled with shame for glory: drink thou also...the cup of the Lord's right hand shall be turned unto thee, and shameful spewing shall be on thy glory.

Someone may get drunk in order to have some sort of sexual encounter or sin. Their will becomes broken down, and they fall into sin.

People believe drinking is such a little thing, but Proverbs 20:1 says, "Wine is a mocker, strong drink is raging: and whosoever is deceived thereby is not wise."

"Well, I drink a little wine for my stomach's sake," you may say. I doubt that you do it for your stomach. I think you drink a little wine for a buzz, or you do it to be accepted socially. But God says that wine is a mocker, and it's raging. Why? Because it brings a curse.

Proverbs 31:4-6 talks about leadership:

It is not for kings, O Lemuel, it is not for kings to drink wine; nor for princes strong drink: lest they drink, and forget the law, and pervert the judgment of any of the afflicted. Give strong drink unto him that is ready to perish.

Leaders shouldn't drink—not even socially—because they never know when they're going to be called upon to act in an emergency, and their actions can affect the whole nation.

There are two ways of looking at Proverbs 31:6: "Give strong drink unto him that is ready to perish." One is to say, "That man is dying. Give him a drink to revive him. Get his heart pumping and stimulate him." I guess that's not so bad, but there are better ways to perform CPR!

The other way to understand Proverbs 31:6 is to say, "That man doesn't care much about life. Give him another drink so he'll slip into unconsciousness and eventually die. It looks like drinking has already killed his liver and his heart and his ambition, and there's not much left of him anyway. He's ready to give up and die, so let him have another drink." I pray that you'll never get to that point of self-destruction that you'll drink yourself to death. Either way, alcohol is not good for the healthy man!

Proverbs 23:20 says, "Be not among winebibbers; among riotous eaters of flesh." Don't even run around with people who drink. Isaiah 5:11 says:

Woe unto them that rise up early in the morning, that they may follow strong drink; that continue until night, till wine inflame them!

What's going to happen if you continue to drink and drink and drink? Not only will it kill you, but what's worse, you will have put a curse on your family and your descendants.

Breaking the Curse of Alcohol

Before you read any further, if you are fighting an alcohol problem that goes back generation after generation, stop right now and pray aloud this prayer:

"Dear heavenly Father, You love me! You sent Your Son to break this curse from my past generation and from me. This alcoholic curse is going to stop this very moment. By faith I proclaim that never again will I have this problem.

"I give this alcoholism to Jesus. Jesus, set me free! I have the name of Jesus, and I am under that name. That name covers me. That blood cleanses me right now, and I am free by the blood. In the name of Jesus, amen."

Now make this declaration of faith out loud:

"Satan, you and your evil spirits of alcoholism have heard my prayer right now! You've had your chance, but your power is broken. Never again will I—nor anyone in my house—ever be a slave to alcohol. In Jesus' name, your curse is broken. Your interference in my life is stopped right now.

"I once was an alcoholic, but now I am delivered. The family curse is broken. None of my children, my grandchildren, or my great-grandchildren—no one in my family—will ever be an alcoholic because the blood of Jesus Christ has cleansed us today and for always. So, devil, get out of here!"

When you've finished your confession of faith, remember to thank and praise Jesus often for His blood and His deliverance. Don't worry if the devil continues to attack you with this temptation. Remind him that Jesus has set you free from the curse of alcoholism. And if you need to, talk to your pastor or someone in your church; many churches have programs that help people overcome addictions with the Word of God. Finally, be faithful to tell others where your "cure" from alcoholism came from: the mercy seat where the blood of Jesus was spilled out for you!

SEXUAL SIN IS A CURSE

Another sin that can bring generational curses upon a family lineage is sexual sin. God destroyed Sodom and Gomorrah for the sin of homosexuality. From whom did the inhabitants of Sodom and Gomorrah descend? They descended from Canaan. As we saw in the last chapter, Canaan was the first homosexual, and homosexuality was what the people of Sodom and Gomorrah were involved in.

You can follow the lineage of the Canaanites all the way down through Joshua's day, and they were involved in sexual sins. They committed all sorts of perverse acts: homosexuality, lesbianism, sex with animals, sexual activity in front of idols.

There are curses that come down to attack a generation, and they have to be broken for them not to continue. You must break the family curse! You may have grandparents or parents or children who are involved in sexual sin—but you don't have to be defeated by it! The devil would like to put that family curse on you, but you can break its power over you and your family.

If you resist it, the devil may try to put it onto your children. Suddenly your children reach the age of twelve or thirteen, and you think, *What happened to this sweet little thing?* It does not have to be that way! Through the power of Jesus Christ, no generational curses need remain in our family lineage.

$$\boxed{3}$$

SIN OR INIQUITY?

We have already seen that iniquities are passed from generation to generation. We have seen how certain hereditary traits which seem to "run in the family" may have originated from just one person who practiced a certain sin until it became a lifestyle or stronghold in that family tree. Once entrenched, the sin became an iniquity—a weakness, bend, or predisposition toward a certain behavior. As that person continually yielded to the temptation of that sin, the demonic forces that influenced him gained dominance in his soulish realm where the mind, will, and emotions are located, and they began to control that individual and, consequently, his future generations.

THE PHENOMENA OF A GENERATIONAL CURSE

One person...

Practices a certain sin . . .
(alcoholism, violence, sexual sin, etc.)

Until...

It becomes a lifestyle.

Once entrenched...

The sin becomes an iniquity—
a weakness toward a certain behavior.

That behavior is practiced over and over...

Allowing Satan to gain control of the mind, will, and emotions.

That control will continue for that individual
and consequently future generations, becoming a...

Generational Curse.

Chart 3

This phenomena is known as a family iniquity or generational curse. If you search the Scriptures, however, you will quickly discover that a family is not the only thing that can be dominated by a generational iniquity; nations, the priesthood (church leadership), and land can also inherit curses.

LAND INIQUITIES

First, let's look at the latter: land iniquities. Second Samuel 21:1 says there was a famine in the land for three years. David went to God in prayer: "God," he said, "something is wrong because You promised us abundance. Is there something spiritually wrong that is holding back Your blessings?" God said, "Yes, it's because of the sins Saul committed against the Gibeonites. Their blood cries, 'Vengeance!' from the ground to Me."

When David asked the Gibeonites what kind of retaliation he should pay, they asked that seven of Saul's sons and grandsons die for what their grandfather had done. The Gibeonites hung Saul's seven descendants. Rizpah, the mother of the men condemned, interceded so that her sons would have a decent burial. David buried her sons with Saul and Jonathan. After the land was cleansed with blood, the famine ended.

Some years ago, a man wrote to me and told me about his farmland. He said a certain kind of weed came up every year, which poisoned the cattle if they ate it. He said that it was all over his land and he had to pay for crop dusters to spray the land every year. It was very expensive and aggravating.

One day he heard that his land might be cursed. His grandfather had bought the land from Indians, and it was rumored that some underhanded things had been done to them. So the Indians put a curse upon it. Once the farmer heard this, he and his wife began to pray. They fasted and prayed and drove around the land and repented of the iniquities of their fathers and grandfathers. They applied the blood of Jesus to cleanse the land.

The next year the weeds came up as usual. But when their son pulled one up, he discovered that the root system was drying up; those few weeds that did come up were withered at the roots. They haven't had that weed problem since. The curse on their land was broken by repentance, acknowledging the sin and applying the blood of Jesus.

As we saw in the Garden of Eden, the curse entered the world when Adam and Eve transgressed God's command. God pronounced a curse upon them, the land, and their future generations. (Gen. 3:16-19.) Since God's final command to Adam and Eve was to "be fruitful, multiply, and replenish the earth," the nations and leadership that came out of Adam's loins were made subject to the effects of their fall as well.

NATIONAL INIQUITY

Ah sinful nation, a people laden with iniquity, a seed of evildoers, children that are corrupters: they have forsaken the Lord, they have provoked the Holy

**One of Israel unto anger, they
are gone away backward.**

Isaiah 1:4

*A national iniquity
is a sin such as
genocide, abortion
or idolatry in which
a nation as a
whole is involved.*

A national iniquity is a sin such
as genocide, abortion, or idolatry in
which a nation as a whole is
involved. For example, abortion,
political or religious corruption, and
pornography are just a few of the
national iniquities that plague the United States.

The wisest man who ever lived, Solomon, began a national
iniquity in the nation of Israel that eventually led to its downfall:

**But king Solomon loved many strange women,
together with the daughter of Pharoah, women of the
Moabites, Ammonites, Edomites, Zidonians and
Hittites; of the nations concerning which the Lord
said unto the children of Israel, Ye shall not go in to
them, neither shall they come in unto you: for surely
they will turn away your heart after their gods... And
he had seven hundred wives, princesses, and three
hundred concubines: and his wives turned away his
heart. For it came to pass, when Solomon was old,
that his wives turned away his heart after other gods.**

1 Kings 11:1-4

How tragic! Because of his inordinate appetite for what the
Bible terms "strange" women, Solomon's heart was turned from

worshiping the true and living God to idolatry: the worship of the creature instead of the Creator. God warned Israel repeatedly not to intermingle with people from other nations. This was not because God was selfish and wanted the Israelites all to Himself but because God understood the mystery of iniquity, that the sins of the fathers are passed on to the third and fourth generations— even nations!

First Corinthians 5:6 says, "A little yeast works through the whole batch of dough" (NIV). As Solomon practiced idolatry, his sin became an iniquity and was inherited by his son, Rehoboam, his grandson, Abijam, and finally the nation of Israel. The entire bloodline had been corrupted:

> **And Rehoboam the son of Solomon reigned in Judah.... And Judah did evil in the sight of the Lord, and they provoked him to jealousy with their sins which they had committed, above all that their fathers had done. For they also built them high places, and images, and groves, on every high hill, and under every green tree.**
>
> **Now in the eighteenth year of king Jeroboam the son of Nebat reigned Abijam over Judah.**
>
> **And he walked in all the sins of his father, which he had done before him.**
>
> **1 Kings 14:21-23; 15:1,3**

Psalm 119:133 says, "Order my steps in thy word: and let not any iniquity have dominion over me." The psalmist was

crying out for God to prevent any individual, family, or national
iniquity from dominating him. He wanted to be free! We know
that God is faithful, and that He has provided a way of escape
from all iniquities through the shed blood of His Son, Jesus
Christ. One of the first steps to individual, family, or national
cleansing is to confess that family or national iniquity:

**If we confess our sins, he is faithful and just to
forgive us our sins, and to *cleanse* us from all
unrighteousness.**

1 John 1:9

NATIONAL CLEANSING

The Bible is our roadmap or blueprint for every situation
we may encounter. The same holds true for families and nations.
By examining biblical examples of how the nation of Israel was
set free of its national iniquity, we can see what we should do
today. In Daniel 9, Daniel goes into a time of fasting and prayer.
He confesses the sins of his fathers and includes himself in the
prayer as well. He prayed and fasted for twenty-one days:

**O Lord, the great and dreadful God, keeping the
covenant and mercy to them that love him, and to
them that keep his commandments; *we have sinned,
and have committed iniquity,* and have done wickedly,
and have rebelled, even by departing from thy
precepts and from thy judgments.**

Daniel 9:4,5

When I look at Daniel, I think, *Daniel didn't sin; his fathers did!* The Bible says Daniel was a very godly man who prayed three times a day. He received the revelation of King Nebuchadnezzar's dream and was delivered by God from the lion's den.

Daniel was highly esteemed by God. He was called the "beloved of the Lord." Why did he include himself as being guilty of the national iniquity? Because he understood the mystery of iniquity—the sins the fathers had passed from generation to future generations. He knew that Israel's seventy-year captivity was almost over. God had told them through Jeremiah that at the end of seventy years they would return to Jerusalem, rebuild the temple, and He would restore their land. The seventy years were almost over, but there were no signs that their captivity was ending. The iniquity of the nation had not been confessed nor had the bloodline been cleansed.

Daniel knew that he was a part of the iniquities that held them in bondage. Because he confessed the sins of the nation's forefathers, God moved to bring them out of Babylonian captivity. He brought in the Medes and the Persians, who diverted the Euphrates River, came under the wall, and took the city. The new king, Cyrus, signed a decree and said that the Jews could return to Jerusalem to rebuild their temple and their nation. But this didn't happen until *after* Daniel had confessed his and Israel's national iniquity in prayer.

Sometimes we may have to look back through our family tree. We may say, "My grandparents and father had temper tantrums, and I do too. God, forgive them, wherever and however these tantrums began. Forgive them and forgive me. Cleanse our family tree with the blood of Jesus!" That is when the curse is broken!

Nehemiah is another example of someone who repented for the nation. He was burdened because he knew that although the temple had been rebuilt, the walls of the temple were still down. He knew that as long as they were down, the Israelites would not live in Jerusalem. He interceded to God on Israel's behalf:

> **I beseech thee, O Lord God of heaven, the great and terrible God, that keepeth covenant and mercy for them that love him and observe his commandments: let thine ear now be attentive, and thine eyes open, that thou mayest hear the prayer of thy servant, which I pray before thee now, day and night, for the children of Israel thy servants, and confess the sins of the children of Israel, which we have sinned against thee: both I and my father's house have sinned.**
>
> **Nehemiah 1:5,6**

Nehemiah confessed the sins of his fathers. "Oh, God," he pleaded, "have mercy on us!" Nehemiah could have said, "I didn't do anything wrong! I don't have to confess the things that they did." But he recognized the mystery of iniquity at work in his bloodline and realized he had the same bend his fathers and the nation of Israel were guilty of, and he cried, "God, forgive us for our national sins and what we have done! We are guilty! Forgive us and cleanse us with the blood!"

After Nehemiah's prayer, the king of Persia let him go back to rebuild the walls and the gates and made provision for building supplies. They finished building in fifty-two days, and Israel's most prosperous time came during the next four hundred years. Why? Because if you cover your sins or the sins of your family, you will not prosper:

He that covereth his sins shall not prosper: but whoso confesseth and forsaketh them shall have mercy.

Proverbs 28:13

If you confess your sins, you will prosper. Nehemiah didn't try to cover or deny his family's or national iniquities. Likewise, we need to humble ourselves and pray over the sins that have been committed in America. We need to include ourselves, because that's when healing can come.

In Nehemiah 9, the entire congregation repented for their iniquities. God healed their land and cleansed them:

If my people, which are called by my name, shall humble themselves, and pray, and seek my face, and turn from their wicked ways; then will I hear from heaven, and will forgive their sin, and will heal their land.

2 Chronicles 7:14

This is a very simple remedy to iniquity. Confess the iniquity and accept the cleansing of the blood. Isaiah 53:5 tells us Jesus was bruised for our iniquities. He carried our sins. He was wounded for our transgressions and by His wounds we are healed. But without His wounds we, and our nation, are still lost in our sins!

Peter saw this when Simon, a sorcerer who appeared to be saved, asked to purchase the gift of the laying on of hands for people to receive the baptism the Holy Spirit:

> **And when Simon saw that through laying on of the apostles' hands the Holy Ghost was given, he offered them money, saying, Give me also this power, that on whomsoever I lay hands, he may receive the Holy Ghost. But Peter said unto him, Thy money perish with thee, because thou hast thought that the gift of God may be purchased with money.... For I perceive that thou art in the gall of bitterness, and in the bond of iniquity.**
>
> **Acts 8:18-20,23**

Peter said, "I see that you are in the bond of iniquity. You still have the iniquity of greed holding on to you." Simon repented and asked Peter to pray for him because he did not want to be bound by greed. Sometimes an iniquity can hold on to you; confess it and take the cleansing of the blood and be set free.

FAMILY INIQUITY

Jesus talked about corrupt trees and good trees and how to prune both. The axe has to be put to the root in order for your family tree to bring forth good fruit. If you study the families of the Old Testament, you will find that God had divine destinies

> *. . . when a family gets into sin, it can avert the plan God has for them.*

for them. The family names were important, as well as their geographic locations. Even the type of food each family produced was divinely purposed by God.

Consequently, when a family gets into sin, it can avert the plan God has for them. When we looked at iniquity, we saw that it is a practiced sin that becomes an inclination in that person's heart. The devil has a plan for your family—a plan of sin. Because iniquity can be passed to the next generation, it can destroy God's divine destiny for that family, and the devil's destiny will occur instead.

JACOB'S WRESTLING MATCH

When Jacob wrestled with the angel in Genesis 32, the angel asked him, "What is thy name?" (v. 27). That question was embarrassing to Jacob because he had been practicing the same sin and trespass over and over again. Even his name, which means *supplanter,* speaks of a person who is not to be trusted. He was a conniver, a schemer, and a deceiver.

Jacob answered the angel, "Oh, I'm Jacob." He hated to say it, but when he admitted he was of questionable moral character, the angel said, "Your name is no longer Jacob, it's *Israel,* meaning 'Prince of God.'" From this example, we see that the only way to get free of sin, trespass, and iniquity is to confess them. It is only then that God can turn you, your family, or your nation from a "Jacob" into an "Israel."

Jeremiah 14:20 says, "We acknowledge, O Lord, our wickedness, and the iniquity of our fathers: for we have sinned against thee." God prospers His people when they confess not only their iniquities, but the iniquities of their fathers.

None of us like to think that what we do has a direct effect upon our children. We like to feel independent about our actions and assume that our attitudes and behavior only affect us. However, Exodus 20:5 assures us that our iniquities will be passed on to our children, our grandchildren, and even to our nation!

ACHAN'S TRANSGRESSION

When the Israelites entered the Promised Land, they were told not to take any spoils from the battle of Jericho. One of the Israelites, Achan, disobeyed, however, and stole a Babylonian garment, two hundred shekels of silver, and a wedge of gold and hid them. When the Israelites fought their next battle—even though no one but God knew what Achan had done—they lost the battle. (Josh. 7.)

God told Joshua that there was sin in the camp, and Joshua called the people to repent. Through Joshua, God gave Achan the opportunity to repent and put a stop to what would happen to him and his family. But he didn't. As a result, Achan and his entire family were stoned:

> **And Joshua, and all Israel with him, took Achan
> the son of Zerah, and the silver, and the garment,
> and the wedge of gold, and his sons, and his
> daughters, and his oxen, and his asses, and his sheep,
> and his tent, and all that he had: and they brought
> them unto the valley of Achor.... And all Israel stoned
> him with stones, and burned them with fire, after
> they had stoned them with stones.**
>
> **Joshua 7:24,25**

The sin of Achan was visited upon the children. That was a
great tragedy, but it is a picture of what 2 Thessalonians 2:7
refers to as the mystery of iniquity which is in operation from
generation to generation. Had they not been killed, that "bend"
toward covetousness in their family would have been passed
down to future generations and may have grievously affected the
nation of Israel. Repentance and cleansing of the blood would
have changed this.

PRIESTLY INIQUITY

In Numbers 16, we read about a man named Korah who
rebelled against the leadership of Moses and Aaron. If you go
back and study the family tree of Korah, you'll see he was
assigned to be the worship leader for the tabernacle. His family
tree was to produce worship and praise and was a part of the
priestly family that took care of the tabernacle. God had a divine
assignment for his family, but Korah decided that he was more

spiritual than Moses and Aaron and that his family should be in
leadership instead.

He began to plant seeds of rebellion and caused others to
rebel against Moses and Aaron. Moses didn't retaliate; instead
he prayed. After he prayed, God caused the ground to open and
swallow Korah:

> **And it came to pass, as he** [Moses] **had made an
> end of speaking all these words, that the ground
> clave asunder that was under them: and the earth
> opened her mouth, and swallowed them up, and their
> houses, and all the men that appertained unto
> Korah, and all their goods.**
>
> **Numbers 16:31,32**

What a shame! Korah's family tree and destiny were
swallowed up because his pride and rebellion became an
iniquity. However, not all of Korah's family tree was destroyed.
His sons did not stand with him in his rebellion. They decided
that just because their father was following the path of iniquity,
it didn't mean they had to follow suit. They were not into
ancestor worship.

Because Korah's sons chose not to stand with their father,
they were not swallowed up by the earth. If you follow their
lineage, you'll see that their descendants became worship
leaders in David's tabernacle and in Solomon's temple, the latter
of which is one of the seven wonders of the ancient world.

As you read the Bible, you will see that the sons of Korah
were worship leaders from generation to generation. Psalm 42

was written by one of the sons of Korah, and we are aware of at least eight other psalms that were written by them.

Korah's sons sought after righteousness and did not yield corrupt fruit. They made a decision to be godly and to follow God's divine destiny for them. The devil would have liked to have destroyed that family with iniquity. Although Korah didn't repent of his rebellion, his sons did, and they were free to fulfill what God had planned for them.

Israel's first king, Saul, and his son Jonathan are another example of a family tree in which a father was corrupt but the son chose not to follow that path of family iniquity. When Saul later came after David with great anger and jealousy and tried to kill him, Jonathan protected David. That is admirable because that iniquity in Saul could have been passed to Jonathan.

Saul and Jonathan both eventually died in battle. But Jonathan had entered into a covenant with David, and a family blessing had been established. After David assumed his kingship, he inquired about Jonathan's seed because he wanted to bless his family line. David tracked down Jonathan's lame son, Mephibosheth, restored to him the lands that had once been Saul's, and allowed him to eat at the king's table every day.

Why did David bless Mephibosheth? Because of the covenant relationship he had with his father, Jonathan. When you sow good seed in the kingdom, you begin a generational blessing. Instead of choosing the iniquity of his father, Jonathan chose the blessings of God, and the next generation of his family reaped the benefits.

THE SONS OF AARON

Aaron, the first priest in the Old Testament, had four sons, two of whom got drunk and offered strange incense before the Lord. The fire of God devoured them. God told Aaron not to even mourn their deaths because what they did was so wrong. Their iniquity could have destroyed the priesthood of Aaron. But his other sons were godly, and the Aaronic priesthood as a whole was good. Their family did not allow iniquity to continue because Aaron accepted God's reasons for destroying his sons.

Eli, the priest, did just the opposite. God had warned Eli about his sons' behaviors. They were not only whoremongers, but they desecrated the offerings the people brought to God and were defiling Him in their eyes. Eli failed to do anything about it, so when their iniquity "was full," God cut off Eli's bloodline. God's divine destiny for them was the priesthood, but their iniquity destroyed them.

Like national curses, family iniquities, and land curses, a priestly curse must be broken through repentance. Because Eli didn't repent, the iniquity went from generation to generation and finally destroyed Eli's entire family tree. Eventually, God will destroy iniquity because it becomes worse with each generation. The way to break a curse is to acknowledge the iniquity, repent, and accept the blood of Jesus to cleanse it.

4

TRACING THE ROOT SYSTEM
OF YOUR FAMILY TREE

The foundation of every plant or tree is its root system. If you examine the roots of some plants, you'll notice that the initial roots are almost microscopic. As the plant continues to grow, however, the roots become thicker and darker until over a period of time, depending on the type of plant, they could become limbs thick enough to swing on.

The same is true for the family tree and family iniquities. The problem you or a loved one may be experiencing right now in the area of anger, depression, or even a health problem may have originated at the beginning of your family's root system generations ago—with a great, great, great-grandfather, who had a tendency to sin.

WAY DOWN DEEP

> *The problem you or a loved one may be experiencing right now in the area of anger, depression, or even a health problem may have originated at the beginning of your family's root system.*

The iniquities of your forefathers are often like evil seeds that are planted deep within the soil of your soul—your mind, will, and emotions. Sometimes they are planted within you before you are even born. Other seeds are planted throughout your early childhood experiences. Some seeds may remain dormant and never sprout. Others, given the right environment, sprout and become strong trees that produce evil or undesirable fruit.

When you act upon and nurture these weaknesses inherited from your family tree, the seeds often become overwhelming, full-grown trees, producing fruit of controlling and compelling evil in your life.

What is the source of the evil seed? Jesus gives us the parable of the wheat and the tares in Matthew 13. He compares the kingdom of heaven to a man who sows good seed in a field, but the enemy sows tares or evil seeds among the good. What Jesus is telling us is that, at this time on the earth, the children of God coexist with the children of the devil. The devil is the one who plants evil seed, and generational curses are another work of his.

Once you understand who is behind the evil work that is being passed from one generation to the next, you will come to realize that the most effective way to kill a generational curse is to cut that tree at its roots—below the surface of the ground. If you can cut the roots and destroy them, the tree will die. Otherwise, the iniquity, like any vegetation, will sprout and grow once again.

What are the roots to the evil tree? Where did they come from? How are they destroyed? John the Baptist had the answer to this question when he said:

> **And now also the axe is laid unto the root of the trees: every tree therefore which bringeth not forth good fruit is hewn down, and cast into the fire.**
>
> **Luke 3:9**

You will find the roots to your family tree's iniquities in the sins and iniquities of your forefathers. This may be difficult for some people to accept because of their love for their family. I love my family, too, but that doesn't mean I'm going to be enslaved by their iniquities.

WHAT'S THAT ODOR COMING OUT OF YOUR CLOSET?

The evil tree represents the bond of iniquity that you may find in your life. The fruit on the tree represents habitual sins or iniquities. These are areas of repeated failure and spoiled fruit. Some evil fruit may exist in your life whether you have participated in the iniquity or not. For example, you may have homosexual tendencies but have never acted upon them.

It's time to bring those hidden sins and iniquities out of the closet and to the forefront. To uncover the root system of your

UNCOVERING THE ROOT SYSTEM
OF YOUR FAMILY TREE

Father
What sins, habits, or
failures do I know of in
my father's life?

_____

_____

_____

Mother
What sins, habits, or
failures do I know of in
my mother's life?

_____

_____

_____

Father's Father
What sins, habits, or
failures do I know of in
my grandfather's life?

_____

_____

Mother's Father
What sins, habits, or
failures do I know of in
my grandfather's life?

_____

_____

Father's Mother
What sins, habits, or
failures do I know of in
my grandmother's life?

_____

_____

Mother's Mother
What sins, habits, or
failures do I know of in
my grandmother's life?

_____

_____

Chart 5

family tree, begin with your parents. Draw a diagram of a tree. Be sure to include enough roots and branches for all of your family members. Then begin with your father. Ask yourself, "What sins, habits, or failures do I know of in my father's life?" If you have problems looking at your dad from this perspective, remember that our purpose is not to condemn or expose him but to correct some problems in your own life.

Make a list of his sins and iniquities. Then ask yourself the same question about your father's parents, listing these traits as well. After you have covered your father's side of the family, then examine your mother's side in the same manner. Again, it is important to look at the sins and the iniquities of the forefathers in relation to the fruit on the tree. As the sins and iniquities of the forefathers are listed, you may discover additional areas of iniquities in your own life.

To take the steps for deliverance, you need to determine as clearly as possible where the roots of the fruit you see on your tree come from. The evil fruit in your life came from somewhere. Don't forget to include physical afflictions in your inventory. Ask the Holy Spirit for help. Ask Him to reveal to you things that are hidden. As you review your legacy of iniquity, take as much time as you need and write down your findings, because if you are vague and don't believe for anything in particular, then you are not going to receive anything at all. To get specific results, you need to pray specifically.

Even if you are adopted or don't know anything about your parents or grandparents, just list the generational curses that

EXAMPLES OF
GENERATIONAL CURSES

Sterility

Divorce

Adultery

Rebellion

Debt

Physical Curses

Arthritis

Cancer

Heart Problems

Kidney Problems

Diabetes

Chronic Pain

Chart 4

you are aware of in your own life. You can be sure that these characteristics had their beginnings in the sins of your forefathers.

After the diagram of your tree is completed, one of two things will happen: you will either be amazed by the reality of the evil tree and its significance, or the overall picture may trigger the realization of additional "fruit in your life" of that evil tree.

SPOILED FRUIT

You may discover that there are a number of generational iniquities at work in your own personal life as well. Some specific curses include: sterility (Deut. 28:18); divorce and adultery (Deut. 28:30); rebellion or loss of your children (Deut. 28:32); and debt (Deut. 28:44). Even your home or property could be under a curse (Deut. 28:38-42).

There are also physical curses that are passed down in the bloodline. Disease often develops as a direct result of sin in a person's life. Some research, for example, has linked arthritis, kidney, and gallbladder problems to the sin of bitterness and unforgiveness.

You can also be cursed by the words someone speaks over you. These are curses that anyone in authority speaks over the life of another. This could include parents, grandparents, physicians, teachers, and even religious leaders su   ~~stors. Word curses such as, "You're so stupid," attack th an individual and can be inherited by the next ge

SYMBOLISM AND TYPES OF GENERATIONAL CURSES

Both the Bible and literature use symbolism to give the reader a picture or mental image of a person, place, or thing. It has been proven that if you can visualize or form a mental picture of something, then you are more likely to remember it.

What do these symbols have to do with the root system of your family tree? They may illuminate to you certain traits of family iniquities. Let me explain. Throughout the Bible, God uses animals as symbols. When God gave dreams to the prophets of old, many times those dreams were a picture "language" to them.

Jesus is depicted throughout the Bible as the Lion of the tribe of Judah. Unlike the devil, who walks about "as a roaring lion seeking whom he may devour (1 Peter 5:8)," Jesus is the real King of the jungle. Scripture refers to Him as King of Kings and Lord of Lords.

My husband, Wally, and I once traveled to Zimbabwe, Africa. We noticed that the people in that part of Africa had what they called "totems." These totems are symbols of their tribes. For example, there was one tribe that had a totem of a snake. Each snake had its own house and one was kept in the backyard of every family in that tribe. The tribal belief was that at night, their god—the snake—left the totem and returned before daylight.

The snake in the Bible and in America is anything but a god. I'm sure that when many of you think about the nature of a snake, you think of a sneaky, crafty, slimy creature. But in some

African countries, they won't as much as touch a snake because they consider it a deity!

THE LIZARD

The lizard is a fearful animal. It moves quickly and jumps at the slightest movement or noise; it is afraid of everything. I know people who are like that—they are so filled with fear that they will flee at the drop of a hat.

Some of my family members are like this. I believe there is an "iniquity" of fear upon my family. Many of them are fearful of what could happen or what the future holds. They wonder if something will go wrong and they will lose everything they've worked so hard to obtain. I've seen this pattern of thinking in my parents, grandparents, myself, and my children.

Do you feel like fear is an iniquity in your family? Would you say that if there were a totem in your backyard, it would be that of a lizard?

BLIND AS A BAT

Have you heard the expression, "They only come out at night"? That is very true of bats, and the reason why is that these nocturnal creatures are blind.

Many families live in spiritual darkness. No matter what you tell them, how hard or often you witness to them, they just cannot see the light of God's Word. Even in the midst of a crisis that would bring most families to their knees, a family who is blind to spiritual things will be oblivious to what is going on. It's almost like there is an invisible wall that perpetuates their dwelling in darkness. No wonder Paul said:

> **Hearing ye shall hear, and shall not understand; and seeing ye shall see, and not perceive: for the heart of this people is waxed gross, and their ears are dull of hearing, and their eyes have they closed; lest they should see with their eyes, and hear with their ears, and understand with their heart, and should be converted, and I should heal them.**
>
> **Acts 28:26,27**

The word *gross* in this context means to thicken or render callous. In other words, the spiritual blindness began when someone in the bloodline rejected the Gospel of truth and hardened his heart to the things of God. This led to spiritual blindness and an iniquity which is passed from generation to generation.

I remember the husband of a friend of ours and how blind he was to spiritual things. You could take him to the most anointed church service, and he'd never get anything out of it. It was almost as though the Gospel was beyond his natural comprehension. His father and grandfather were the same way.

Because of the condition of their hearts, this family will remain in darkness until someone in their family tree comes into the saving knowledge of the Lord Jesus Christ. The devil works in darkness. But when the light comes, the darkness is dispelled and the devil is revealed for who he is—a defeated foe and a liar. Psalm 119:130 says, "The entrance of thy words giveth light; it giveth understanding unto the simple." Once the power of darkness is broken over a family, they can be set free of spiritual blindness.

THE SNAKE

The snake has always been a symbol of lying and deception. From Genesis to Revelation, Satan is depicted as a liar and deceiver. As a matter of fact, his first appearance in the Bible was in Genesis, when he deceived Adam and Eve in the Garden of Eden in the form of a snake. In a family tree, the snake is symbolic of the destructive tendencies of lying and deception.

Racial and ethnic prejudice is a deception that has become an iniquity in families and nations. Many wars have been and are being fought along racial and ethnic lines. And it runs deep. I remember when I was just six years old and I overheard my grandparents make a racial comment. I dearly adored them, but when I heard their comment, something inside of me said, *This is wrong*.

They were being deceived by the devil because of their own racial prejudice. That deception was passed to their children and grandchildren. Thank God it was not passed to me. I chose not to allow that same pattern of family iniquity.

THE OWL

The owl has been used as a symbol of wisdom and knowledge. I can remember our local library used to encourage us to read, and the owl was the symbol on the bookmarks they'd give us. The owl in a family tree represents false knowledge.

The first recorded sin in Scripture was that of seeking after knowledge. Eve was tempted to eat of the Tree of Knowledge of Good and Evil. The serpent told her that if she would eat of the tree, she'd become as a god, knowing good from evil:

And the serpent said unto the woman, Ye shall not surely die: for God doth know that in the day ye eat thereof, then your eyes shall be opened, and ye shall be as gods, knowing good and evil. And when the woman saw that the tree was good for food, and that it was pleasant to the eyes, and a tree to be desired to make one wise, she took of the fruit thereof, and did eat, and gave also unto her husband with her; and he did eat.

Genesis 3:4-6

I know a young lady who was raised in satanism. She was dedicated to Satan as a child, and her head was filled with false knowledge about him. When her mother and brother became born again, they started bringing her to church. She'd sit in the service as though a dark cloud were over her head. She had the look of death on her.

Even though she'd get headaches each time she attended a service, she continued coming until one night, the light of God's Word penetrated the darkness that had this woman bound. Today she is one of the most radiant Christians in our church. She was set free from the occult and the false knowledge that Satan is god.

THE VULTURE

The vulture is an unclean bird. We associate the vulture with dead animals. We know that by nature, it eats creatures that have already died and begun to decay. This bird is shown in the death scenes of many old western films. You see it circling in the air, hovering over its dying victim, waiting to descend so it can eat its flesh.

In a family tree, the vulture is a symbol of tendencies that are associated with death. These tendencies include both suicidal and homicidal predispositions.

Suicide and murder have become common occurrences in today's society. I'm sure you've either heard of or perhaps lived in communities where suicide or violence seemed to run in certain families. I've heard of a family in which the mother overdosed on pills, her son committed murder, and the grandson committed a murder/suicide. How tragic! But this is just one of the many iniquities that can be found in a family tree.

THE FROG

The frog is symbolic of carnal or sexual sin in a family tree. In nature, frogs are known for their multiplication and jumping. Some people are just like frogs—they jump into situations without thinking, and some even jump from bed to bed.

With the HIV virus and the threat of AIDS being at an all-time high, I'm sure many of you would agree that sexual sin runs rampant throughout the world. Pornography and homosexuality have almost become commonplace. This iniquity has become so entrenched in the fabric of American society that both the American family and the nation as a whole are affected by it.

Sexual iniquity in a family tree is a strong sin to deal with because it literally enslaves the members of each generation:

> **Know ye not, that to whom ye yield yourselves servants to obey, his servants ye are to whom ye obey; whether of sin unto death, or of obedience unto righteousness?**
>
> **Romans 6:16**

> **Know ye not that he which is joined to an harlot is one body? for two, saith he, shall be one flesh.... Every sin that a man doeth is without the body; but he that committeth fornication sinneth against his own body.**
>
> **1 Corinthians 6:16,18**

The Egyptians were very much involved in sexual sin. Some of the animals they worshiped had to do with the types of sexual sins they committed. God judged the Egyptians with the plagues he sent to destroy them. Many family trees are completely wiped out because of their sexual sin. This does not have to happen to your family tree, however; God has provided a way of escape through repentance, forgiveness, and the shed blood of Jesus.

THE SPIDER

The spider is known for the webs it spins. No matter how well you clean your house, you'll find a spider in some remote corner of your home. If you get rid of the web but don't destroy the spider, it will spin a web in another spot in your home. Spiders are very territorial. With each web they communicate, "This turf is mine, and I'm not going to share it."

One of the strongest and most dangerous webs that a person can weave is possessiveness. The spider in the web in a family tree is symbolic of greed, selfishness, and jealousy.

The Bible says that "the love of money is the root of all evil" (1 Tim. 6:10). Greed, selfishness, and jealousy feed off of one another. Greed breeds selfish behavior: "I want it all to myself and refuse to share with anyone else. There's only enough for me!" Once greed and selfishness team up with one another, then jealousy kicks in. "You have more than me, and I want what you have too."

America is full of greed. We're not a team-oriented society; everything is "Me, me, me, me." Greed is a strong, inherited trait in most family trees because success and material well-being are equated with money. To most people, it doesn't matter how you make your money, just as long as you have a lot of it.

Many a family has been destroyed because of this iniquity. And like the spider and her web, this family trait cannot be eradicated by simply destroying the web (the symptom); the spider (the root) must be destroyed as well. Otherwise, it will simply go to another part of your home—the next generation of your family tree—and spin an even bigger, stronger web.

THE SCORPION

The scorpion is a creature that inflicts great pain. It is symbolic of a tendency toward pain. This tendency in a family tree could be in the form of self-pity.

There are many people who have a tendency to dwell upon the emotional hurts and pain of their past. They have a "woe is me" attitude and get great satisfaction out of licking their wounds. If you attempt to tell them that Isaiah 53:4 says Jesus has already born their griefs and carried their sorrows, they will become upset with you. After all, you can't possibly understand how bad they've been hurt and are still hurting—they say.

Many Christians are living with emotional pain from their past—some simply through ignorance and some by choice. The good news is that Christ won their freedom over two thousand years ago and by His stripes, they are free!

THE HORNET

Hornets also inflict pain, but they are better known for their anger and aggressive attacks. In a family tree, they are symbolic of anger, rage, bitterness, and revenge.

People who have this kind of iniquity in their family tree are likely to become angry at the drop of a hat. They are very negative

SYMBOLISM AND
GENERATIONAL CURSES

 Lizard   Fear

 Bats   Spiritual blindness or darkness

 Snake   Lying and deception

 Owl   False knowledge

 Vulture   Suicidal or homocidal tendancies

 Frog   Carnal or sexual sin

 Spider   Greed, selfishness or jealousy

 Scorpion   Self-pity, tendency toward pain

 Hornet   Anger, rage, bitterness and revenge

 Turtle   Laziness and procrastination

Chart 6

people who are either always angry with someone or always looking for someone else to hate. They have very few friends. You can see the anger raging from generation to generation.

THE TURTLE

Are you as slow as a turtle? This animal is considered by many as one of the slowest moving animals God made. It sticks its head in its shell when trouble comes. Some families are like turtles: they get very little accomplished. They often shirk responsibility when they need to assert themselves. The turtle symbolizes both laziness and procrastination in a family tree.

PRAYER OF CONFESSION

Each of these unclean creatures is representative of a tendency toward sin that you may find in your life or in your family tree. By now I'm sure you're beginning to understand that we all have inherited certain family iniquities. I'm sure you're also beginning to realize that you and your future generations can be free to walk in blessings you've inherited from Jesus through His death, burial, and resurrection.

Through the finished work of Jesus Christ, you have the authority to declare that the generational curses in your family are broken!

SECTION 2

*The Valley of
Blessings and Cursings*

5

WRITTEN IN STONE

Deuteronomy 27 and 28 is one of the most interesting portions in the Bible because it shows God's people putting His Word into action, and it compares His blessings with some terrible curses that will occur if His Word is not followed.

Before Moses turned the leadership of the children of Israel over to Joshua, he instructed them very carefully. Then, when Joshua took the Israelites into the Promised Land, they followed Moses' command and turned themselves into a living Sunday school lesson.

Following Moses' instructions, Joshua divided all of Israel into two groups. One group he sent over to Mount Gerizim, and the other group he sent over to Mount Ebal. To the priests or Levites in the first group, he gave a long list of blessings; and to the priests or Levites in the second group, he handed a long list of curses. Then Joshua conducted the two groups like an orchestra leader.

The first group shouted out the first blessing on their list, and the people answered, "Amen"—or "I understand." Then the second group shouted out their first curse, and the people answered, "Amen" or "I agree." This went back and forth, and the people eventually had to decide which they liked better, the curses or the blessings. Which would you choose?

> **And the Levites shall speak, and say unto all the men of Israel with a loud voice, Cursed be the man that maketh any graven or molten image, an abomination unto the Lord.**
>
> **Deuteronomy 27:14,15**

Anybody who got involved in idolatry was in a cursed position. Idols bring curses. People who get involved in witchcraft or in a cult can pass that sin down from generation to generation.

THE WITCH'S CURSE

Once we saw a Baptist-made movie about a young man who was being witnessed to by a group of Christians. This young man wanted to be saved, but his mind was terribly attacked. It seemed that his grandmother was a witch, and she had put a curse on him. He couldn't receive the Lord because he was blinded by this curse.

But the Christians stood against the curse. The devil got mad and said, "I have killed the grandmother, and I've killed the mother in this family. Now I'm going to kill this boy." The evil spirit even said what time he was going to kill the boy.

The Christians continued to stand against the curse. They watched the clock, they spoke the Word against the curse, and they prayed. At the hour when the boy was supposed to die, the curse was broken, and he received Jesus as his Savior! I like the lesson of that movie: Curses are awful, but they *can* be broken.

DIFFERENT CURSES

The Bible lists different kinds of curses. There were curses on people who cursed their family:

> **Cursed be he that setteth light by his father or his mother.**
>
> **Deuteronomy 27:16**

People who rebel against their parents bring a curse on themselves, and that curse can be passed from generation to generation. Don't rebel against your parents. It doesn't matter what they're doing; you'll bring a curse upon yourself and pass it on to your children—and you don't want that to happen!

Then there is a curse of cruelty:

> **Cursed be he that maketh the blind to wander out of the way.**
>
> **Deuteronomy 27:18**

There are people who are actually cruel and violent. I saw a true story on television about a mother who killed her own child, and I thought, *Oh, how terrible!* When they checked out that mother's background, they discovered that she had been abused by *her* mother. Obviously she hadn't been killed by her mother, but the sin got worse as it progressed from one generation to the next. The mother had inherited the weakness from her mother, and the evil spirits tempted her. She fell into that iniquity, committing a worse sin than had been done before.

Sexual sin seems to be one of the very worst curses. Deuteronomy 27:20-23 talks about all kinds of sexual sins that bring curses. Sometimes people act like it's not a big deal to have an affair, but it will become a big deal when the devil robs you of everything you've got. Immorality is a big deal. It's a curse; it's sin. It hurts you, and it will hurt your seed!

The last part of Deuteronomy 27 — verses 24 and 25 — has to do with violence. Violence is a curse, and anyone who enjoys committing, watching, or condoning violence is under a curse. Keep away from it! Don't promote it! And don't pass it on to your children.

FREEDOM FROM CANCER

There are all sorts of generational curses we haven't even dealt with yet. One of the biggest that needs to be discussed is cancer.

If you have a family history of cancer, then pray this prayer to break that curse of cancer:

Dear heavenly Father, I come to You in the name of Jesus. I thank You that Jesus paid that price, that Jesus took the cancer, and I don't have to have it. I reverse the curse in Jesus' name. My children will never have cancer, and their children will never have cancer and their grandchildren will never have cancer. The curse is broken! In Jesus' name, amen.

Now thank Him every day of your life that He already paid the price; He already shed His blood so you won't ever be subject to cancer. The more often you speak that word of positive confession, the more often the devil will also hear you saying it to the Father, and he'll not be able to get an inroad into your life or in your children's lives.

Oh, yes, the devil can hear you standing on God's Word! He can hear you praising Jesus every day for breaking the curse of cancer from your life. It makes him so mad.

In Deuteronomy 27 and 28, God told the Israelites what the curses were and what the blessings were. He said, "If you do these things, you're going to be cursed." He wanted to be sure the people really understood it, that it was tied to their hearts. That's why when they read the curses off, everybody said, "Amen." And when they read the blessings off, everybody said, "Amen."

The people didn't read it, but they heard it from the priests, and when they said amen to it, it signified that they understood. God knew that these weaknesses from past generations had to be broken. He knew they couldn't sow something evil into their children which would come up and be a curse back.

He not only wanted them to break the *past* generational curse, but He also wanted them to break the *present* generational curse. He said, "If you do righteously, you will be blessed. But if you do wrongly, you're going to bring the curses." So the people said amen to it.

WRITTEN IN STONE

The children of Israel were also to write down the blessings shouted down to them from Mount Gerizim, and they were to write down the curses shouted down to them from Mount Ebal. They wrote down the blessings and curses on stone so they would never be forgotten or destroyed. As the people read the blessings and the curses, they answered, "Amen, amen, amen."

6

THE MERCY SEAT

Now I'm going to give you some good news and some bad news. When we looked at Noah's drunkenness in a previous chapter, we may have said, "Oh, that is just so awful." What happened to Noah? He got drunk. But even when there is sin, "The curse causeless shall not come" (Prov. 26:2). God always makes a way to break that sin.

When Adam and Eve sinned, immediately God made a way to break that sin, to nullify that curse. Genesis 3:21 says:

Unto Adam also and to his wife did the Lord God make coats of skins, and clothed them.

God killed an animal and made them coats of skin. He shed blood because *the blood was the answer to the curse!*

You see, life is in the blood. And once Adam and Eve fell into spiritual death through sin, only the substitute of a blood sacrifice could temporarily atone for their sins.

When Cain and Abel came upon the scene in Genesis 4 they knew all that had gone on before them. They knew about their parents' sin and how God's answer for their curse was blood. But when it came time for the sons to make their own offerings, Cain ignored the blood sacrifice and instead brought the vegetables which he had grown. Abel brought a lamb from his flock because he knew that blood would break the curse.

Cain chose to ignore that there could be a curse for sin, just as there are people today who choose to ignore that sin can bring a curse. The devil tries to tell them, "Well, it might be a curse to so-and-so, but it won't hurt you. You're so sweet and good otherwise—how's one little sin going to harm you?"

That's what Cain said: "I don't believe that I need to shed blood. I don't believe there is a curse." But his brother's sacrifice was accepted, and Cain's sacrifice was not accepted because he refused the blood. Similarly, if you refuse the truth, you'll believe a lie; you'll be deceived.

Cain was deceived, and he killed his brother in a jealous rage. There is no justification for Cain's behavior because he refused to make the blood sacrifice that would have been acceptable to God. God *always* wants to break the curse with the blood!

What breaks the curse for you? The blood!

Whose blood? The blood of the Lamb!

What breaks the curse for your family? The blood!

What breaks the curse of inheriting bad things from the past? Absolutely, the blood of Jesus Christ!

RIGHTEOUSNESS AND JUSTICE

God essentially said, "When you bring the blood, you receive mercy from the curse." Adam and Eve and their children had a place to worship the Lord. They were outside the Garden, but they had a special place where there were two cherubs. This was a foreshadowing of the mercy seat in the temple. These two cherubs represented *righteousness* and *justice*.

When they brought the blood of the lamb and sprinkled it on the mercy seat, they said, "God won't judge us because He sees the blood, and the blood breaks the curse of our sin." That was an example of the mercy seat.

Eventually there was the first physical mercy seat. In Exodus 25 and 26, God told Moses how to make the tabernacle: "Put the ark of the covenant in the Holy of Holies, and it will have a golden lid and two cherubims, and they will face each other...when the high priest goes in on the Day of Atonement, he will sprinkle blood on the mercy seat."

By this, God was saying, "Instead of accounting your sins to you, they are to be judged through the blood sacrifice. I will break the curse through the blood. Justice and righteousness are satisfied by the blood."

In the New Testament, Jesus is the supreme blood sacrifice. When he arose from the dead, the disciples looked in His tomb, and they saw two angels, one at the head where His body lay and one at the foot. What was that indicating? *Jesus is our Mercy Seat. He shed His blood to break the curse!* All righteousness and justice is satisfied because of the blood of Jesus.

There is no reason for us to take a curse physically, mentally, emotionally, or in any other way from a past generation or relationship. Thank God, we're free!

According to Hebrews 9:14, Jesus took His blood up to the Father. Everything which was on earth as "the tabernacle" was patterned after the heavenly tabernacle. (Heb. 9:23.) Jesus took His blood and put it upon the mercy seat in heaven. I can just imagine what happened: He said, "Father, here is My blood."

The Father replied, "Here is the mercy seat. All who come under Your blood are already judged."

THE CURSE OF THE CANAANITES

Many people throughout the Bible have ignored the blood and fallen under the curse. When we looked at Noah and his lineage, we saw that Cain's seed kept getting into sin. Lamech was another whose seed produced generations of iniquity. The sin came down in those generations, and nobody broke it with the blood.

Noah was forgiven of his drunkenness because he made a sacrifice. He took the blood, and the blood spoke mercy. That satisfied righteousness and justice for what he had done.

But the Canaanites kept getting into sin, and those evil spirits were attacking each generation, saying, "That's my house! That's my house!"

How did they ever get out of sin? Well, they *did* get out of sin, but not in a good way.

God told Joshua, "When you go in to take Canaan, kill them all. I don't want any of them because there are so many generations of sin, and it has to be broken. Sin is contagious, and I don't want you catching it."

They were Cain's cursed generations. Noah had stopped the curse, but Canaan revived it. So finally God decided to kill all the Canaanites when their iniquity was "full." (Gen. 15:16.) God told Joshua to do it. It was God's command to kill them all.

Why? Maybe they had AIDS. I wouldn't be surprised because if they had homosexuality, lesbianism, and sexual activity with animals for generation after generation, who knows what diseases they must have had by that time!

Twenty-four thousand Israelites got involved with the Midianites, and they all died in a day. Their sin was a very serious thing. Sin brings a curse.

Joshua and the Israelites were ready to go into the Promised Land and kill all the Canaanites at God's command. But there was a woman named Rahab, who was a Canaanite and a prostitute. She had committed all kinds of sexual sins herself, and she had inherited sexual sin from previous generations. But somehow she got a hold of God's Word, believed it, and broke the curse!

Know therefore that the Lord thy God, he is God, the faithful God, which keepeth covenant and mercy with them that love him and keep his commandments to a thousand generations.

Deuteronomy 7:9

Not only did she break the curse for herself—she broke it for her future generations. "They that love Me, I will bless them to one thousand generations." (Ex. 20:6.)

That means you say to the devil, "You don't get my children, you don't get my grandchildren, you don't get my great-grandchildren. If Jesus tarries, you don't get anyone who belongs to my house for a thousand generations! This curse will not go on. It will stop in Jesus' name."

That's how Rahab stopped the curse. How do we know that God blessed her future? Rahab married a Jew, and she had a baby. She named that baby Boaz. Boaz married Ruth, who became the mother of Obed. Obed had a son named Jesse; Jesse had a son named David, and David became the king. Jesus is a direct descendant of King David; therefore, Rahab is in the lineage of Jesus Christ!

We can go down a thousand generations and see Rahab as blessed. What was her past? She was a Canaanite and a prostitute—but she broke the curse!

When the Israelites came in to fight the Gibeonites, there was a similar story, found in Joshua 9 and 10. The Gibeonites were Canaanites, but they came under the blood. They were deceivers, rapists, liars; even their name means a snake. But they said, "We want your God." When they did that, they broke the curse.

Ruth was another example. She was a Moabitess, and her genealogy was terrible. But when she came to the Lord, what happened? She came under the blood sacrifice, and the blood broke the curse. The blood can break any curse.

THE NAME ABOVE ALL NAMES

Blessed be the Lord God of Shem...God shall enlarge Japheth, and he shall dwell in the tents of Shem; and Canaan shall be his servant.

Genesis 9:26,27

After reading that verse, you might say, "Oh, poor Noah. That grandson of his, Canaan, produced such a bad line." But there were three sons: Ham, Shem, and Japheth. Of Shem the Bible says that his brothers would dwell in his tent. This means that both brothers and all their descendants would come under Shem's tent, or be covered and protected by him. Of course, Ham's descendants—Canaan and his seed—were servants to Shem's descendants because of the curse. They were not equals or inheritors of the blessing.

The word *Shem* means name.[1] What was Noah actually prophesying when he said, "They will come under Shem's tent"? He was saying, "They will be protected by Shem—or by the *name*."

89

The Jewish race came through the descendants of Shem. Noah was saying, "There will be a *name* that even Canaan can run under and find protection!" And who would be the name that would come through Shem? Who is their very own Messiah? Who is the name above all names? *Jesus!* Jesus became a curse for us that we might be blessed! (Gal. 3:13.)

When something rises up in your household, you need to rebuke that curse. Then you can tell your children, "I've blown it; I've sinned. That's a curse, but the devil is not going to put it on you. I've repented of it. I've received mercy and righteousness through the blood of Jesus. Now don't you get into the same curse just because I did. You are saved from the curse!"

Once we cast an evil spirit out of a woman. We asked the evil spirit, "Why are you in there?" The evil spirit answered, "Because if I get her, I can have her kid too." The devil doesn't tell the truth very often, but I think he told it right then.

We rebuked that spirit, saying, "You can't have her kids because you can't have her!" That woman was delivered.

Six or seven years later she came to our church. She said to me, "Do you remember me?"

I answered, "Do I remember you? I'll never forget you!" It was with her that I had my first experience with casting out demons! Glory to God—we broke that generational curse!

She said, "We belong to Jesus, and He belongs to us—and so does our family!"

TERRY'S STORY

There was a man in our church who had a terrible background of alcoholism. His name was Terry, and Terry's testimony is beautiful. I'll let him tell it in his own words:

"In our family there were five boys. Including my dad, all the men were alcoholics. Dad was from Hazard, Kentucky, where you either worked in the coal mines or sold moonshine for a living. My father drank vodka for fifty years, but during the last year of his life, all Dad wanted to do was watch preachers on TV and go home to be with Jesus.

"I didn't live long with my oldest brother, Darrell. He was a lot older than me. When I was only about four or five years old, he was already an alcoholic. I remember when I was little watching him knife-fight behind the house in an alley. But when I saw him a year ago, I sat down and talked with him. All Darrell wants to talk about is what God is doing in his life. There is nothing else important to him.

"My next brother—who is four years older than me—was an alcoholic who went to Vietnam in the war. When he came back, all he did was drink. But the last time I saw him, he had married a Pentecostal preacher's daughter from Middletown, Ohio, and now they take turns preaching on Sunday.

"I've got a brother a year older than me. He had a pretty rough time of it. He couldn't escape his drinking problem. God is really working in his life; we've seen a lot of things break off of him. He's going to heaven, too, but he just doesn't know it yet.

"I went into the hospital about six years ago. I was so drunk when we filled out the admission papers that I didn't even know what year I was born in or whether I was married or not.

"A nurse took me aside one night and said, 'Now, Terry, you've just got one chance. When was the last time you prayed?'

"'It's been a long time ago,' I answered.

"'Why don't you pray now?' she asked. For about fifteen or twenty minutes, I told her how I wasn't good enough to ask God for help. She said, 'You tell your Father that, and know the God of your understanding.' [Ex. 35:31.]

"I answered, 'Well, I can do that.' So I went into my room, got down on my knees, and told God how I wasn't good enough. I said, 'You can take me if You want to. I don't want any halfway job done.

"'But if You do take me, I'll do what You say from here on out.' I ended that prayer the way I had been taught: In the power of Jesus' name.

"I got up off my knees knowing that I was never going to drink again. I knew it then, and I haven't drunk another drop since then, not in six years.

"You might be somebody who was as sick as I was. You don't have to drink anymore if you're willing to let God run your life daily. I've talked with people who are alcoholics and people who have grown up in homes with alcoholics. There are even people who've been coming to church for five, ten, twenty years, and you know that they've got a bottle rattling back there.

"Maybe you've been drinking since you were a kid, or maybe it's somebody in your family or one of your kids who drinks.

"God has been dealing with you about drinking for a long time. Don't be deceived. The devil isn't that strong; we give him more power than he deserves.

"The other kind of person is one who has grown up in an alcoholic home or has married an alcoholic and perhaps later divorced. You're doing all you can do to walk with the Lord and keep His ways. But there is always something there that just keeps at you and keeps at you, and you can't figure out what it is. Don't be deceived any longer. God has got a plan for you too.

"My family once lifted up a 'vegetable' in prayer— me—and stood on the Word of God, and I came back as a complete miracle! I am the result of prayer. My whole

family is a miracle! We were all alcoholics—and now we're all saved."

Terry came to the mercy seat, and through the blood of Jesus, he broke the curse of alcoholism in his life—and he kept the curse from continuing into the next generation.

God makes a way for you to break *any* curse in your life or in the lives of your children: Simply come to Him with the blood of Jesus, the acceptable sacrifice that atones for the iniquities in our lives and any generational iniqutites we may have inherited.

7

INHERITED CURSES

Generational, or inherited, curses used to bother me terribly. I thought, *Now wait a minute! I don't want to have to answer for my great-grandfather's sin!* It's enough to answer for and deal with your own sins.

But there is a law in nature called the law of culpability. The word *culpability* means "responsibility for wrong or error or blameworthy."

The Scripture says that all shall answer for their own sins. They will be accountable to God for their sins, but that weakness in an area of their lives—physically, mentally, or emotionally—is transmitted to the next generation and possibly the generation after that. And it happens because "**...of them that hate me**" (Ex. 20:5).

Let's review a little. Deuteronomy 27 and 28 told us all about the curses and the blessings. As the curses were read out, everybody—the men, the women, the children, the grandmothers, and the grandfathers—heard them, and they answered, "Amen, so be it." God wanted them to know that sin brings a curse. He wasn't trying to be hard on them. He wanted to be good to them so they wouldn't bring curses on their lives.

Perhaps it seems strange to you to confess the sins of your parents. You're probably thinking, *Marilyn, I've never heard of this before*. The following Scriptures are only a few of the many that deal with this subject, but they will establish your heart in this almost forgotten biblical principle:

> **If they shall confess their iniquity, *and the iniquity of their fathers*, with their trespass which they trespassed against me, and that also they have walked contrary unto me...then will I remember my covenant.**
>
> **Leviticus 26:40,42**

> **And the seed of Israel separated themselves from all strangers, *and stood and confessed their sins, and the iniquities of their fathers*.**
>
> **Nehemiah 9:2**

> **We acknowledge, O Lord, our wickedness, and the iniquity of our fathers: for we have sinned against thee.**
>
> **Jeremiah 14:20**

Proverbs 26:2 says, "The curse causeless shall not come," or to paraphrase, "When there is a curse on a generation, it didn't just happen to occur; there has to be a cause behind it." What is always the cause behind the curse? Sin. Sin is what always brings the curse. Any time there is a curse in a person's life, there is some root of sin.

Let me give you another example. When I visited with my aunt, I asked, "What was my grandfather like?"

She answered, "Let me tell you about your great-grandfather first. He would get drunk once a year, and then he would beat his animals. There were a lot of good things about him, but there was one bad thing: He was cruel to his animals."

Then she went on to say that my grandfather had that same kind of cruelty. In my family, we've seen that cruelty occur again and again. As we discussed in the last chapter, cruelty is a curse. When you are being cruel or unkind or hateful to somebody, you are operating in a curse.

We've already discussed the specific curses mentioned in Deuteronomy 27 and 25. Now let's look at curses which are inherited.

DROUGHTS AND DISEASES

The Lord shall make the pestilence cleave unto thee, until he have consumed thee from off the land, whither thou goest to possess it. The LORD shall smite thee with a consumption, and with a fever, and with

an inflammation, and with an extreme burning, and with the sword, and with blasting, and with mildew; and they shall pursue thee until thou perish.

Deuteronomy 28:21,22

Disease, and your enemy coming after you, would be a part of sin. When people sinned in the Old Testament, they broke the law, and then the curse could overtake them.

Then God also talks about drought, a lack of rain:

And thy heaven that is over thy head shall be brass, and the earth that is under thee shall be iron. The Lord shall make the rain of thy land powder and dust: from heaven shall it come down upon thee, until thou be destroyed.

Deuteronomy 28:23,24

He was saying, "If you fall into idolatry and get into sin, you will cause drought and famine."

When the Israelites fell into idolatry under Ahab and Jezebel, Elijah prayed, "God, don't let it rain for three-and-a-half years." When the people repented, the fire from heaven fell. Then Elijah prayed, and he watched and waited—and the rain came. Why? When the people repented, they reversed the curse. The way to break the curse is by repentance.

Now how did Elijah stop the rain from falling in the first place? He used the Scriptures. He didn't get mad at Ahab and Jezebel and just spitefully say, "I'm going to stop it from raining." He simply prayed the Word of God:

**As the Lord God of Israel liveth, before whom I
stand, there shall not be dew nor rain these years,
but according to my word.**

1 Kings 17:1

He said, "I've gone to the Word," and he prayed the Word,
and he stopped the rain. Then he prayed the Word and broke the
curse because the people repented, and the rain came again.

HEREDITARY ILLNESSES AND PROBLEMS

Heredity can be defined as "the genetic transmission of
characteristics from parent to offspring; the totality of
characteristics and associated potentialities transmitted to an
individual by heredity."[1]

There are generations of families who suffer nothing but
defeat. Wally and I know a family in which the grandfather was
defeated, the father is defeated, and the two children of that
family are defeated. One of the children died of cancer, and the
other son is full of fear. I hate to think what will happen to the
grandchildren and further on in generations to come.

There are certain family diseases:

**The Lord wilt smite thee with the botch of Egypt,
and with the emerods, and with the scab, and with
the itch, whereof thou canst not be healed. The Lord**

shall smite thee with madness, and blindness, and
astonishment of heart.

Deuteronomy 28:27,28

The "botch of Egypt" is boils and tumors; tumors are a form of cancer. Madness and astonishment of heart are confusion of mind and amnesia; these are mental illnesses.

Blindness is glaucoma, cataracts, near-sightedness, far-sightedness, and all other eye diseases. Have you ever seen a family in which every single one of them wears glasses? From the father and mother down to the littlest child, all wear glasses, usually those really thick-lensed kind. Those poor people are under a curse, and they need to be set free from it!

Then God talks about poverty:

Thou shalt not prosper in thy ways: and thou
shalt be only oppressed and spoiled evermore, and
no man shall save thee. Thou shalt betroth a wife,
and another man shall lie with her; thou shalt build
an house, and thou shalt not dwell therein: thou
shalt plant a vineyard, and shalt not gather the
grapes thereof.

Deuteronomy 28:29,30

"Well, I come from a family in which nobody knows how to handle their finances. No one ever taught me how to save money or to tithe or to be thrifty." We're talking about more than just careless habits or a lack of sound teaching—we're talking about being under a curse!

Another current example of the curse of poverty is the huge number of home repossessions going on in today's economy. Verse 30 predicts this as well: "Thou shalt build an house, and thou shalt not dwell therein."

And in many families, immorality is rampant: "Thou shalt betroth a wife, and another man shall lie with her" (v. 30).

Here's what can happen: the alcoholic father takes his paycheck to the closest bar and drinks it all away. So his wife starts fooling around with the next door neighbor because her husband is never home.

Then there's a divorce; the abandoned wife is left with all the children and rarely does she get any child support. Those children grow up with their mother's having one boyfriend after another, and they hardly know who their father is.

> *Poverty breeds immorality, shame, carelessness, and crime.*

Poverty breeds immorality, shame, carelessness, and crime. The curse starts in one generation and just grows and grows, making itself worse with each new generation. Where did that curse come from? Proverbs 26:2 tells us there is always a cause, so there must have been sin!

BREAKING THE CURSE OF HEREDITARY DISEASE

Let me give you some real-life examples of inherited curses. Several years ago I was teaching on the subject of healing at a

Bible study in a home in Denver. A certain woman happened to attend this particular Bible study.

During the teaching she just wouldn't sit down, and it bothered me. I thought she was antagonistic toward the Bible study. Afterward I talked with her, and she said, "Well, you may say that healing is for today, but I don't believe it." Then she told me about two very desperate needs she had.

Her father was blind. He had a hereditary eye disease that would usually strike each family member when they were in their early thirties. Their eyes would gradually get worse and worse, until by the time they were in their forties, they were completely blind.

This woman was in her mid-thirties, and she was starting to go blind. But even worse than that, her teenage daughter was beginning to go blind too. This was a generational curse!

I didn't know about generational curses at that time, but the more knowledge we get, the more we know how to attack the enemy and set people free:

> **My people are destroyed** [perish] **for lack of knowledge.**
>
> **Hosea 4:6**

This woman was literally perishing, and so was her daughter. She didn't believe what we were studying, but she needed that healing desperately. And not only was she losing her sight, but I discovered that the reason she had been standing throughout the Bible study was that her hip bone had been operated on and part of the bone had been removed. She hadn't been able to sit comfortably for a very long period of time. She needed healing badly!

A well-known evangelist was coming to town, and some of the people in the Bible study invited this woman to go with them to his meetings, but she refused. But then her daughter said, "Mother, it can't hurt to go just one time." So she and her daughter went.

They were sitting in the balcony of the auditorium, and the evangelist called out for people who had problems in their hips or in their bone structure. The daughter said, "Mother, stand up! It couldn't hurt."

It certainly didn't hurt. She felt the warmth of the Lord go all over her. She knew something had happened, but she didn't know how to identify it.

That night as she was getting ready for bed, her daughter came in the bedroom and was talking with her. The daughter said, "Mother, there's an extra lump on you." The bone had been removed, so nothing showed. The daughter said, "Mother, feel for yourself. I think you have a hipbone now!"

The mother felt her hip, and she had a new hipbone! God had done a miracle! Her spirit caught on fire after that!

She came back to the Bible study and said, "I believe in healing! I believe in healing!" She told us her story, and then she said, "Now I want you to pray for my eyes."

We rebuked the devil and prayed for her eyes—and she has 20/20 vision today! And her daughter who was going blind is not blind today because the generational curse was broken!

FIGHTING THE STRONG MAN

So how do you put a stop to so-called familiar spirits that visit your family with generational curses? You bind the strong man. Matthew 12:29 says:

Or else how can one enter into a strong man's house, and spoil his goods, except he first bind the strong man? and then he will spoil his house.

In this Scripture, the word *house* can mean generation. (Matt. 10:6.) In order to break the curse of the generations before us—their habits, their sins, their physical weaknesses—we must go in and bind the strong man who has brought that curse down to us from past generations.

So who is this "strong man"? It is Satan, of course. What do we have to do to him? We must bind him. Then we take the *house*—or that generation—away from him!

We say, "Hey, devil, wait a minute! My generation doesn't belong to you because I bind you in the name of Jesus!" We break that curse in the name of Jesus.

When awful things start to occur, we say, "I'm not going to have heart problems. I'm not going to have diabetes...I'm not going to be an alcoholic...I'm not going to have a weakness for immorality because my mother was involved in that...I'm not going to abuse my kids because I was beaten, or there was incest, or I was molested! That curse is not going to come on me. I'm not going to do it to my children, and my children are never going to do it to their children!"

Why? "Because I break that curse, and I bind that strong man. The curse of my generations is broken!"

But if you think you're going to tell the devil to "get lost" just once, you're wrong! He'll come back and attack you again and again. You've got to get serious.

This is an important lesson for young people. When the devil comes to you with immorality, that is a curse. Girls, when some guy wants something from you that you shouldn't be giving him, that's a curse. And, guys, when some girl tries to tempt you, that's a curse. If you get into immorality, you will bring a curse on yourself, and on your children, and on your children's children. Don't do it. Don't get involved. Be smart.

"SEVEN OTHER SPIRITS"

Matthew 12:43-45 tells us:

When the unclean spirit is gone out of a man, he walketh through dry places, seeking rest, and findeth none. Then he saith, I will return into my house from whence I came out; and when he is come, he findeth it empty, swept, and garnished. Then goeth he, and taketh with himself seven other spirits more wicked than himself, and they enter in and dwell there: and the last state of that man is worse than the first.
Even so shall it be also unto this wicked generation.

This is in the same chapter as the instruction on binding the strong man. When we defeat the devil the first time, we can be sure he's going to try again!

Here's what it says: "When the unclean spirit is gone out of a man, he walketh through dry places, seeking rest, and findeth none." So we see that the devil had been cast out. "Then he saith, I will return into my house...." The devil thinks that *your house*— your generation, your seed, your children—belongs to him!

That makes me so angry! The devil has the audacity to think that my house is his house! But my house does not belong to the devil. My house—my generation, my family, my children, my grandchildren—belongs to the Lord!

But what happens when the devil returns? When he comes in, he finds the house empty, swept, and garnished. You see, my house has been all cleaned up by Jesus. The Holy Spirit came in and threw out all the old junk and completely redecorated the whole place.

But what does the devil do then? He takes "seven other spirits more wicked than himself, and they enter in and dwell there: and the last state of that man is worse than the first. Even so shall it be also unto this wicked generation."

We're talking about generations, about families. The devil will come in and attack your children with the old weaknesses and the old sins that you had...or your grandmother had...or your great-grandmother had. He'll go after your kids, and they'll be worse than you were—unless you bind the strong man in Jesus' name.

Why is this generation so bad? Sin is the worst we've ever seen it because the evil spirits have come with seven times more to attack. Whenever there has been a cleansing, they come after the kids to make them seven times worse. You'd better believe it: *the devil is after your children.* But he doesn't get them because *your house is not his house.* Don't you dare let him take them! Don't let your kids get into alcohol or drugs or immorality or any of that other garbage. Jesus came to set us free and to keep us free, and our houses belong to the Lord!

> *The devil will come in and attack your children with the old weaknesses and the old sins that you had...or your grandmother had...or your great-grandmother had.*

FAMILIAR SPIRITS

Now, your generation may have been cleansed, but your children have got to walk in cleansing too! The curse has to be broken from them, too, or they will inherit the weaknesses from you which came from your father, your grandfather, and your great-grandfather. What does the devil do? He watches for those new generations so he can attack them too.

The Old Testament talks about "familiar spirits":

Regard not them that have familiar spirits...to be defiled by them: I am the LORD your God.

Leviticus 19:31

And the soul that turneth after such as have familiar spirits...I will even set my face against that soul, and will cut him off from among his people.

Leviticus 20:6

What are familiar spirits? They are fallen evil spirits that become familiar with a family. They follow that family with its weaknesses—physical, mental, emotional sin—all the way down each generation, attacking and tempting each member in that way because they already know that they have a weakness for it.

> *What are familiar spirits? They are fallen evil spirits that become familiar with a family.*

If your father was an alcoholic, those evil spirits will watch you. They know that you probably already inherited a weakness for alcohol, and they'll try to drive you crazy with that addiction. If you have children, they'll watch for the next generation to attack them too. They are familiar with your family from generation to generation, and they try to get each generation into sin so they can carry the curse on from there.

SAUL AND THE WITCH OF ENDOR

An example of familiar spirits is given in the account of the witch of Endor. (1 Sam. 28.) Saul went to this witch because he had totally blown it with God. He had sinned, and he had not repented. He could have reversed his curse if he had admitted his sins to God.

God could have turned his situation around just as He could have with Cain, and with Esau, Jacob's brother who gave away his birthright for a meal. (Gen. 29:29-34.) But they didn't repent of their sins; it was always somebody else's fault. With Saul it was David's fault. With Esau it was Jacob's fault. With Cain it was Abel's fault. They didn't get their cleansings because they were too busy making their cop-outs!

And when Saul saw the host of the Philistines, he was afraid, and his heart greatly trembled. And when Saul inquired of the Lord, the Lord answered him not, neither by dreams, nor by Urim, nor by prophets. Then said Saul unto his servants, Seek me a woman that hath a familiar spirit, that I may go to her, and inquire of her. And his servants said to him, Behold, there is a woman that hath a familiar spirit at En-dor. And Saul disguised himself, and put on other raiment, and he went, and two men with him, and they came to the woman by night: and he said, I pray thee, divine unto me by the familiar spirit, and bring me him up, whom I shall name unto thee.

Then said the woman, Whom shall I bring up unto thee? And he said, Bring me up Samuel. And when the woman saw Samuel, she cried with a loud voice... And the king said unto her, Be not afraid: for what sawest thou? And the woman said unto Saul I

saw gods ascending out of the earth. And he said
unto her, What form is he of? And she said, An old
man cometh up; and he is covered with a mantle.
And Saul perceived that it was Samuel... And Samuel
said to Saul, Why hast thou disquieted me, to bring
me up?

And Saul answered, I am sore distressed; for the
Philistines make war against me, and God is
departed from me.... Then said Samuel, Wherefore
then dost thou ask of me...? Because thou obeyedst
not the voice of the Lord, nor executedst his fierce
wrath upon Amalek, therefore hath the Lord done
this thing unto thee this day. Moreover the Lord will
also deliver Israel with thee into the hand of the
Philistines: and tomorrow shalt thou and thy sons be
with me: the Lord also shall deliver the host of Israel
into the hand of the Philistines.

1 Samuel 28:5-8,11-16,18,19

Saul couldn't face the truth, and he was deceived. If you
refuse the truth, you will believe a lie. He went to see the witch
at Endor to find out if he was going to win the battle or not. The
witch called up a spirit, but I do not believe that it was Samuel.

It looked like Samuel, it talked like Samuel, it had a mantle
like Samuel's. It said, "Why did you cause me unrest? I was
very much at peace. I'm going to tell you what's going to
happen to you. Tomorrow you and your household are going to
be killed."

Witches don't call us out of graves. Jesus does. He called Lazarus back from the grave. (John 11.) He brings the resurrection. But the evil spirit who had the appearance of Samuel was a familiar spirit. "How could that evil spirit emulate Samuel so well?" you ask. Because it was familiar with Samuel and his family.

There are all sorts of occult practices going on today. There are people who find somebody who is grieving over a lost loved one, and they will say, "Come in, and we will call that loved one." They knock on tables and do all kinds of strange things. Then some evil spirit enters and says, "I'm Uncle Joe. How are you doing? I miss you too."

Well, it's not Uncle Joe. Those people cannot bring up the spirits of dead people. So what is that spirit? It is an evil spirit that is familiar with Uncle Joe.

If you're doing this sort of thing—playing with Ouija boards and such—then you're involved with a dangerous thing. Flee from anything like that. You do not need to be around familiar spirits or evil spirits. You need to be around the Holy Spirit constantly. And you need to warn your children about it. They should not have any part with it either.

8

THE CURSE OF THE HERODS

In this chapter, we will examine one of the great families in leadership during the time of Jesus' walk on earth. The Herodian family clearly demonstrates how generational curses can take hold and be passed down through a family's lineage.

HEROD THE GREAT

Now when Jesus was born in Bethlehem of Judaea in the days of Herod the king, behold, there came wise men from the east to Jerusalem, saying, Where is he that is born King of the Jews? for we have seen his star in the east, and are come to

worship him. When Herod the king had heard these things, he was troubled, and all Jerusalem with him.

Matthew 2:1-3

Herod "the Great," the king at the time of Jesus' birth, was not fully Jewish. He was partially an Idumean, which is an Edomite, a descendant of Esau. As we have already seen, Esau hated the things of God, and therefore, Herod the Great was part of a cursed generation. (Gen. 25:34; Heb. 12:16,17.)

When you follow the history of the Edomites, you find that they hated the things of God. They were always provoking the Israelites, and there were never good relations between these "cousins." History records that the sons of Esau hated God and the sons of Jacob loved God. There was an ongoing battle between them.

Herod the Great was half-Idumean and half-Jewish. Within his own nature there was a battle between the God-lovers and the God-haters. But God was trying to intervene in Herod's life. God wants to break the generational curse; that is always His will.

In this case God sent the wise men to Herod, and they told him about the Bethlehem star. Herod went to his scribes and asked, "Can you find anything that would help me know if this really is the king of the Jews?"

This is a very supernatural plan of God. The wise men were not Jews, and they weren't Idumeans either. They had come from the Far East, and supernaturally an unusual star had appeared. They were following that star, just it had been prophesied by Balaam:

**I shall see him, but not now: I shall behold him,
but not nigh: there shall come a Star out of Jacob,
and a Sceptre shall rise out of Israel, and shall smite
the corners of Moab, and destroy all the children of
Sheth. And Edom shall be a possession, Seir also
shall be a possession for his enemies; and Israel shall
do valiantly.**

Numbers 24:17,18

The scribes looked it up in the Scriptures and said to Herod, "In the Word it says someone is to be born in Bethlehem and He is to be the King." They actually gave Herod the Word of God, sent to him for his own salvation.

Any time the Word comes, what does it bring? It brings light. What was happening to the darkness of this man? The light of the Word of God was knocking at his door.

But what did Herod do with the light? He refused it. He had the opportunity to break the curse of his generations, but he rejected it! He had inherited generation after generation of curses and sin, but he blew his chance to be set free from the curse. Then he turned and committed an even worse sin—the mass murder of all the Jewish male babies under two years of age: Then Herod...slew all the children that were in Bethlehem, and in all the coasts thereof, from two years old and under (Matt. 2:16).

HEROD ANTIPAS

Herod the Great had a son: Herod Antipas. All of his sons had the generational curse on them because the sins of the fathers then were visited on the children. (Ex. 34:7.) There was therefore a weakness in Herod Antipas. But God always wants to break a curse. It doesn't matter what the weakness is, it doesn't matter how bad the sin is, because repentance and the blood of Jesus will break the curse!

God began to deal with Herod Antipas. (Mark 6:14-28.) Herod had committed a very bad sin: he had married his brother Philip's wife, Herodias. John the Baptist had preached against it, saying that it was wrong.

So Herodias had a fit and said, "Throw him in prison! I don't like him talking about me on the streets!" John probably had called her a prostitute and harlot. So they threw him in jail.

For Herod feared John, knowing that he was a just man and an holy, and observed him; and when he heard him, he did many things, and heard him gladly.

Mark 6:20

But Herod Antipas was touched by John. He called John up out of prison and said, "John, talk to me about spiritual things." Herod was hungry for the things of God! So John talked to him, and you could see that Herod's heart was being turned.

What was God getting ready to do? Break the curse! John gave Herod the Word, the Word brought light, the light began to chase away the darkness. God's light is greater than any generational curse.

But one night Herodias had a big birthday party for Herod, and it was a drunken brawl. She brought out her glamorous daughter, Salome—who was not Herod's daughter but his niece—and she began to dance before him. Herod was very much aroused by this girl, and he said, "I'll give you anything up to half of my kingdom."

So Salome ran to her mother and said, "What shall I ask for?"

Well, Herodias was mad. She answered, "You bring me John the Baptist's head; that's what I want." So Herod Antipas had to stick to his promise, and he cut off John the Baptist's head, even though he felt bad about it. But instead of letting the light overcome the darkness, he kept on progressing in the curse. He was acting in violence and cruelty, just like his father.

But God didn't stop dealing with him. If it were up to me, I'd have thrown some of these people out the window! I wouldn't be like God and try again. I'd say, "Forget it. They're all a mess!" But God isn't like that. He keeps trying to break that family generational curse. So Jesus appeared before Herod Antipas.

By this time, Herod Antipas was a nervous wreck. When Jesus was brought before him in Luke 9:9, Herod, still feeling guilty, asked, "Are you John the Baptist risen from the dead?" When Jesus, the beautiful Savior of mankind, came to Herod before the crucifixion, Herod refused Him. That curse was not broken.

HEROD AGRIPPA

**Now about that time Herod the king stretched
forth his hands to vex certain of the church. And he
killed James the brother of John with the sword. And
because he saw it pleased the Jews, he proceeded
further to take Peter also. (Then were the days of
unleavened bread.) And when he had apprehended
him, he put him in prison, and delivered him to four
quaternions of soldiers to keep him; intending after
Easter to bring him forth to the people. Peter
therefore was kept in prison: but prayer was made
without ceasing of the church unto God for him.**

Acts 12:1-5

I would have said, "Forget it. Hang it up." But God kept
trying for four generations! Here is another Herod, the third one.
This one threw Peter in jail, and he was going to kill him. The
Jews were very happy that Peter was in jail, and Herod had
already killed James.

Herod was thrilled and thought this had added to his
popularity. He was very aware of politics, and evidently he had
not been too popular. But while Peter was in jail, God tried to
deal with this Herod.

God sent an angel who released Peter, and Herod heard of
this tremendous miracle. (vv. 6-10.) At that time, miracles had
been happening in the city, and he knew about them. Any time
the miraculous occurs, God is trying to deal with people. God
gets a lot of mileage out of a miracle.

God was trying to get Herod Agrippa to repent. But this Herod—instead of repenting—murdered the men who were guards for Peter. (v. 19.) He refused the light, holding onto the violence and cruelty which he had inherited from his grandfather and his father. "The curse causeless does not come," does it? But the curse can be broken.

HEROD AGRIPPA II

And as he [Paul] thus spake for himself, Festus said with a loud voice, Paul, thou art beside thyself; much learning doth make thee mad. But he said I am not mad, most noble Festus; but speak forth the words of truth and soberness. For the king knoweth of these things, before whom also I speak freely: for I am persuaded that none of these things are hidden from him; for this thing was not done in a corner. King Agrippa, believest thou the prophets? I know that thou believest. Then Agrippa said unto Paul, Almost thou persuadest me to be a Christian.

Acts 26:24-28

Herod Agrippa II was the next Herod in this family's lineage, and we read about him in Acts 25 and 26. He was the great-grandson of Herod the Great. Herod Agrippa II was called to listen to a man in a courtroom. The man's name was Paul the apostle. God was sending the best of His warriors!

Paul was brought before Agrippa II and said, "King Agrippa, I know you're not ignorant of things." Herod Agrippa must have been stirred and drawn of God. God wanted to turn that whole family around, because it was a family that was making a tremendous impression on the nation of Israel.

Perhaps the saddest words in the Bible, Agrippa's reply was, "Paul, you almost persuaded me to become a Christian." "Almost" is not enough. You are fully persuaded—or you're not in. Herod Agrippa II lost his chance, and he was the fourth generation.

Herod Agrippa II was the last of his family. They were the rulers of their country, but they lost it all. History says that Agrippa lost his position and bought a farm on Mount Vesuvius to live out the rest of his life in shame and exile. But Mount Vesuvius was a bad place to buy a farm, because when it erupted and destroyed all the countryside, that was the end of the Herods.

Throughout the lineage, God dealt with each Herod, and each one rejected Him. He tried with the first generation, and the second, and the third, and the fourth. The sins of the fathers were visited on the children for four generations, and God tried to break the curse at each generation.

Now think about it: have you ever heard or read of another Herod? You never hear about any Herods today. You've never met anybody who has said, "I've descended from those famous Herods back there in Jesus' day." Why? Because they perished; there are no Idumeans (or Edomites) today because they were devoured by the curse. The devil wants to do the same to *your* family line, but God has provided the way to stop the curse and replace it with blessing!

9

JOB AND HIS HOUSEHOLD

Let's examine the life of a man who experienced the devil's curse but who broke it through repentance.

And the Lord said unto Satan, Hast thou considered my servant Job, that there is none like him in the earth, a perfect and an upright man, one that feareth God, and escheweth evil? Then Satan answered the Lord, and said, Doth Job fear God for nought? Hast not thou made an hedge about him, and about his house, and about all that he hath on every side? thou hast blessed the work of his hands, and his substance is increased in the land. But put forth thine hand now, and touch all that he hath, and he will curse thee to thy face. And the Lord said unto

Satan, Behold, all that he hath is in thy power; only upon himself put not forth thine hand.

Job 1:8-12

Job was a man who suffered from bitterness. All the things that happened to him—he lost everything—were not entirely his fault, for God allowed the calamities to come upon him as a test of his heart and as proof to the devil.

At first Job didn't blame God for his troubles:

In all this Job sinned not, nor charged God foolishly.

Job 1:22

But his "friends"—Eliphaz the Temanite, Bildad the Shuhite, and Zophar the Naamathite—began to erode his confidence in God through their "counsel," and Job developed bitterness in his heart.

> *Complaining and bitterness are like Siamese twins: you can't separate them.*

That's why it's so important for you to associate with positive, God-fearing people and not let yourself be pulled down to the level of those who love to wallow in gloom and doom.

Job started to complain. Complaining and bitterness are like Siamese twins: you can't separate them. Complaining is a very dangerous thing to do because you are really saying, "I don't believe God can do anything about this. I don't believe people can change."

To be honest, if I had been Job and had gone through all the things he did, I probably would have been bitter too. He'd lost his children; he'd lost his wealth; he'd lost his health. He also had three wretched friends. Job had these things happen to him, and he said, "I will complain in the bitterness of my soul" (Job 7:11).

Here is where we get into trouble. We say, "I have a right to be bitter." No, you don't; bitterness is simply too expensive!

It goes on: "I will speak in the bitterness of my soul" (Job 10:1).

He said, "I'm so bitter. Things are so hard. It wasn't my fault. Why did this happen? Things are so bad."

"YE SHALL KNOW THE TRUTH..."

When we look at Job's situation, we say, "Poor Job, he had it so hard." But we don't need sympathy when we have it hard. We need the Word to set us free! Sympathy and pity put us in a place that allows our bad situations to perpetuate. But the Word sets us free:

> **Now no chastening for the present seemeth to be joyous, but grievous: nevertheless afterward it yieldeth the peaceable fruit of righteousness unto them which are exercised thereby.**
>
> **Hebrews 12:11**

If you practice godly sorrow, you'll get the "peaceable fruit of righteousness." But if you allow yourself to wallow in earthly sorrow, you're going to be depressed forever. And depression and bitterness are all in the same package.

THE CURSE OF FEAR

What's the other feeling that Job experienced? Fear.

For the thing which I greatly feared is come upon me, and that which I was afraid of is come unto me.

Job 3:25

Fear came upon me, and trembling, which made my bones to shake.

Job 4:14

It looks like Job's weakness was already known to the devil because he was able to exploit that weakness so thoroughly. Job's own fearfulness contributed to the virulence of the curse that the devil brought on him.

Your fear can contribute to a curse entering into your life, but love casts out fear:

There is no fear in love; but perfect love casteth out fear: because fear hath torment. He that feareth is not made perfect in love.

1 John 4:18

Fear is one of the devil's favorite tools because it is so subtle. A little worry can grow into a medium-sized concern, which grows into a huge mountain of fear. When you are weighed down with a mountain of fear, then you won't be much good in spiritual warfare!

I remember a lady who married late in life and had two children. She was a real fussbudget about her kids. Any time one of them would sneeze once or twice, she had the thermometer out and was stuffing him into a sweater. At the first sign of a little rash or puffy eyes, she was wringing her hands and saying, "Oh dear! My little one has a terrible allergy!"

One of the little children heard his mother talking that way, and he began to be very picky about what he would eat. "Oh, I can't eat that because Mommy says I'm allergic to that kind of food," he'd say. Within a short time that little child developed full-blown allergies to certain foods, and those allergies threatened his very life!

I believe that woman worried and fussed and "feared" those allergies into her child's life. She walked in doubt and fearfulness, rather than in confidence in God's Word, and her fear allowed the devil to launch a sneak attack on her family. Her fear was a sin, and sins always bring a curse.

"...AND THE TRUTH WILL SET YOU FREE!"

So these three men ceased to answer Job, because he was righteous in his own eyes. Then was kindled the wrath of Elihu the son of Barachel the Buzite, of the kindred of Ram: against Job was his wrath kindled, because he justified himself rather than God.

Job 32:1,2

With all kinds of terrible things happening to him, Job was murmuring and complaining and protesting to God that he was so righteous. He was full of self-righteousness!

His three friends—Eliphaz, Bildad, and Zophar—even got fed up with his nonstop complaining and his stuffy self-righteousness, and they left him. So God used another young man, Elihu, to speak on His behalf; He gave Elihu the Word of God to bring to Job:

> **But there is a spirit in man: and the inspiration of the Almighty giveth them understanding.... For I am full of matter, the spirit within me constraineth me.**
>
> **Job 32:8,18**

If we get in the Spirit, we will understand things—"the inspiration of the Almighty giveth them understanding" (Job 32:8)—and we'll know how to be set free. As long as we try to handle it in the flesh, we won't get the spiritual revelation of it:

> **Then the Lord answered Job out of the whirlwind, and said, Who is this that darkeneth counsel by words without knowledge? Gird up now thy loins like a man; for I will demand of thee, and answer thou me. Where wast thou when I laid the foundations of the earth? declare, if thou hast understanding.**
>
> **Job 38:1-4**

God Himself came to Job and said, "Who do you think you are anyway? You don't even know one thing about this situation."

JOB AND HIS HOUSEHOLD

Job recognized the voice of God. He didn't get all puffed up and say, "Well, if that's the way God is going to talk to me, I'm going to change churches!" When Job stopped talking about himself long enough to listen, he heard God speaking. Afterward, he said:

Wherefore I abhor myself, and repent in dust and ashes.

Job 42:6

Job didn't say, "I abhor my wife. She's got the sharpest tongue. Why did I ever get stuck with her?" He didn't say, "I abhor my friends. Have you been listening to what they're saying? God, I'm so disgusted. I hope You kick them really hard. I hope You really get them because they came to comfort me, and instead they made me feel worse. So go get them, God!"

No, what Job did say was, "I abhor myself." Does that sound like genuine godly repentance to you? Now, repentance doesn't require self-hatred. Nonetheless, who do we have to repent for? If you don't know how to answer that, then you need to ask the Holy Spirit to show it to you.

THE BLOOD REVERSES THE CURSE

God spoke to Job's three friends and said:

Therefore take unto you now seven bullocks and seven rams, and go to my servant Job, and offer up

for yourselves a burnt offering; and my servant Job shall pray for you.

Job 42:8

When Job repented, watch what God did. He said, "Offer a sacrifice"—because it's through the blood that the curse is reversed—"and pray for your friends."

"Pray for them? I don't want to pray for my friends. Let's burn them for the sacrifice!" No, that's not what Job said. He was repentant and obedient to the Lord. He responded to God's Word. So what happened?

And the Lord turned the captivity of Job, when he prayed for his friends: also the Lord gave Job twice as much as he had before.

Job 42:10

When Job prayed for his friends, his captivity was turned. Do you want your captivity to be turned? Do you want to reverse the curse in your life?

But I say unto you, Love your enemies, bless them that curse you, do good to them that hate you, and pray for them which despitefully use you, and persecute you.

Matthew 5:44

If you want your captivity turned, then you'd better bless those who have persecuted you and spoken against you. You'd better forgive them, and ask God to forgive you for your part in it, because nobody is totally innocent.

When you do that, just watch God turn your captivity! He will turn it around because you have reversed the generational curse. When you do that, something will happen with your seed and with the seed that is to come.

Teach your children: "Don't you get into bitterness. If the devil comes to tempt you with this, you tell him, 'Get out of here! I'm not under the generational curse. I'm under the blessings of the heavenly Father, and I have a new nature.'"

10

FAMILY CURSES
AND BLESSINGS

GOD BLESSED THE FAMILY

G od has always been concerned about the family. In Genesis, He established four divine institutions:

1. The first institution God put into place was free will. (Gen. 2:16,17.)

2. The second institution was marriage. (Gen. 2:18,21-25.) God has always meant for us to marry.

3. The third was the family. (Gen. 1:28.) God made marriage to be the nest to protect the children, to be a place where children are trained up in His ways. They will then go out and reproduce and raise their children

to become Christians and continue the godly lineage from there.

4. The fourth institution was the nations. (Gen. 11:6-9.) After the Flood, God never intended for just one nation to rule the whole world. He intended that there would always be small nations because they would protect individual rights.

> *God established four divine institutions: free will, marriage, the family, and nations.*

God has such unique things planned for the family! He put His blessing on Adam and Eve, and He gave them and their children dominion over the earth. But they sinned, and sin brings the curse.

As soon as they sinned, God made a way out of their sin: through the shedding of blood, He clothed them with the skins of animals. (Gen. 3:21.) Right away, they saw there was a way out from the curse, and they had access to His mercy seat.

ESAU BLEW IT

God then began to show Abraham how He would bless the family. (Gen. 13:14-16.) God gave Abraham tremendous promises for his seed. When his son Isaac came on the scene, God really blessed the family. Then *his* son Jacob came on the scene, and God blessed the family. But Isaac's other son, Esau, blew it:

Also Esau saw that the daughters of Canaan did not please Isaac his father. So Esau went to Ishmael,

and took to be his wife, [in addition] to the wives he [already] had, Mahalath daughter of Ishmael Abraham's son, the sister of Nebaioth.

Genesis 28:8,9 AMP

I've always thought, *Well, Esau blew it because he sold his birthright. He treated the things of God lightly and never did repent of what he had done. Oh sure, he was sorry about the situation—and he wanted to kill Jacob for what he'd done—but he never repented of his own sin. He just got into vengeance.*

But there's something else that Esau did. He married into the Hittites. Esau had two Hittite wives. Isaac and Rebecca were very grieved over Esau's marrying those two women. They had sent Jacob up to Laban to get a wife, but what was the problem with Esau's taking Hittite wives?

After I did some research, I found out that the Hittites were descendants of the Canaanites. There was a curse on the Canaanites, a generational curse that hadn't been broken. So what Esau was doing was bringing that generational curse into his family.

This is why the Bible tells you not to marry a non-Christian: "Be yet not unequally yoked together with unbelievers" (2 Cor. 6:14). Why? Because they are under the curse of sin. Do you want your children to be under the curse? Then don't marry an unbeliever. You want your home to be blessed, not cursed; you want your children to be blessed, not cursed. When you came to Jesus, you began to break that curse. So don't marry an unbeliever and invite a new curse in.

That's why Isaac and Rebecca were so upset. They knew that Esau's marriage to a Canaanite was bringing an unbeliever into their family, allowing the curse into their family.

But God was always concerned to do something to change the family! In Exodus, God was very concerned about the family of Israel, and He always had been. He was concerned about Adam and Eve's family, about Seth's family, about Abraham's family. Why? Because not only curses are passed from generation to generation, but blessings can also be passed down too!

Some of your natural talents and strengths are those you've inherited from your parents. And you've probably gotten some spiritual lessons from a grandmother who prayed for you, or a great-grandfather who stood fast in prayer for you when you were involved in sin. Those are blessings that have come down to you.

THE EGYPTIANS

Now let's look at another "family" God had tried to change but finally had to judge: the Egyptians.

And Moses said, Thus saith the Lord, About midnight will I go out into the midst of Egypt: and all the firstborn in the land of Egypt shall die, from the firstborn of Pharaoh that sitteth upon his throne, even unto the firstborn of the maidservant that is behind the mill; and all the firstborn of beasts. And there shall be a great cry throughout all the land of

Egypt, such as there was none like it, nor shall be like it any more.

Exodus 11:4-6

You know how this story goes. The Egyptians had enslaved the Israelites, and God raised up Moses, an Israelite who was an adopted son of the Pharaoh to be the deliverer of His true people from their captors.

Moses warned Pharaoh again and again of coming judgment, but he kept hardening his heart toward God's people. So the Egyptians suffered plague after plague: frogs, locusts, polluted water, and all sorts of infirmities on the land. But Pharaoh continued to reject God's warnings, and he and his people continued to live under the curse.

Finally, God said, "Now I'm going to judge the Egyptian family." Notice that He referred to a family unit. "I'm going to take the firstborn in every Egyptian family." Why? Because the Egyptian families were under the curse.

The Egyptians were wallowing in sin. They worshiped idols and did not repent at all in spite of the dramatic miracles God brought. God wanted them to repent. He didn't cause the miracles just to get the Israelites out of slavery—He did that too— but He also wanted to bring the Egyptians into His kingdom.

THE BLOOD OF THE LAMB

In the tenth day of this month they shall take to them every man a lamb, according to the house of

their fathers, a lamb for an house...and the whole assembly of the congregation of Israel shall kill it in the evening. And they shall take of the blood, and strike it on the two side posts and on the upper door post of the houses, wherein they shall eat it.

For I will pass through the land of Egypt this night, and will smite all the firstborn in the land of Egypt, both man and beast; and against all the gods of Egypt I will execute judgment: I am the Lord. And the blood shall be to you for a token upon the houses where ye are: and when I see the blood, I will pass over you, and the plague shall not be upon you to destroy you, when I smite the land of Egypt.

Exodus 12:3,6,7,12,13

God said, "So that your family will not be under the curse, you must kill a lamb and put the blood of that lamb over the doorpost of your house." When the angel of death passed over, what did he see? He saw the blood of that lamb, and the blood reversed the curse!

What will save your family today? The blood of Jesus. The solution is not in humanism or psychology. It's not in reading self-help books or in "sparing the rod." The blood of Jesus is what will save your family today.

BEING UNEQUALLY YOKED

"Yes, but Marilyn, what about when you marry somebody before you are a Christian, then become a Christian, and the other person doesn't? So what do you have—a family curse that can't be broken?"

That's not true, and I've got one Old Testament and two New Testament Scriptures to prove it!

> **God setteth the solitary in families: he bringeth out those which are bound with chains: but the rebellious dwell in a dry land.**
>
> **Psalm 68:6**

God is saying, "I'll save one in a family, and that will set those free who are bound with chains. I'll take those out who are rebellious, living in a dry land."

> **And the woman which hath an husband that believeth not, and if he be pleased to dwell with her, let her not leave him. For the unbelieving husband is sanctified by the wife, and the unbelieving wife is sanctified by the husband: else were your children unclean; but now are they holy.**
>
> **1 Corinthians 7:13,14**

One believing mate sanctifies the household. And your children are freed from any generational curse.

> **Likewise, ye wives, be in subjection to your own husbands; that, if any obey not the word, they also**

**may without the word be won by the conversation of
the wives; while they behold your chaste
conversation coupled with fear.**

1 Peter 3:1,2

The conversation or the behavior of the wife will be the
greatest Christian witness any unbelieving husband will ever
see. If it is the husband who is saved, he will love her like Christ
loves the church, and she can't resist the irresistible love of
Jesus Christ shown through her husband!

Sometimes it takes just one to break the generational curse.
You can be that one! Don't you dare give up and say, "Well,
my spouse won't come to church, so I'm going to backslide." If
you do that, you are inviting the generational curse back into
your family—probably seven times worse!

You certainly don't want the curse on you, or on your
husband, or your children, or your grandchildren, or the next
generations. The cost of backsliding is too expensive!

BREAK THE CURSE—OR BE WIPED OUT!

God is very concerned that family curses be broken. That's
why He absolutely wiped out the Herods. He dealt with them
again and again, but they refused to repent. So after the fourth
generation, He wiped them out.

He wiped out the Canaanites. All those "ites" you read about
in the Old Testament—the Amorites, the Hittites, the Hivites—
are all from the Canaanites. God told Joshua, "When you go in,

just wipe out the whole crowd. I dealt with them, and I dealt with them, and they stayed in sin. So I don't want them intermarrying with My people and bringing their generational curses with them." That's why He wiped them out.

I believe many of the problems Wally and I encountered with our adopted son Michael were because we didn't understand generational curses. Many of the problems with your natural-born children are generational curses. When you examine it closely, some of the problems we deal with in ourselves—insecurity, fear, poverty, anger, violence—are the problems your father, or your mother, or your grandmother, or your grandfather dealt with. But you tell the devil that he isn't going to do that to your house!

You say, "This house has been cleansed. The blood of Jesus is over it, and you're not bringing seven other evil spirits in. This is not your house; this is my house, and it belongs to Jesus! Satan, you stop this in the name of Jesus! This house will never be yours!"

A pastor told about what had happened in his family. He said that his daughter was about to get involved in some sin. He took his Bible and read to her the part about the curses, and then said, "Now this is what happens when you get into these things. Is that what you want for your life?" She answered, "No!"

He said, "Well, that's what is happening. These curses have come down upon you, and now is the time for them to stop. Do you want to stop them?" And she wanted to stop them.

We need to tell our children the truth: "Hey, if you curse me and you act rebelliously toward me, you're putting a curse on yourself," or, "If you get into sexual sins, you're putting a curse on yourself."

If you were involved in sin yourself, you might as well level with your kids and say, "I blew it when I was your age, but I don't want this thing coming on you. I had a weakness in this area, but I've repented. And God cleansed me. Now you're not going to have that same tendency in you."

EVERYDAY CURSES

There are some basic curses in the Bible which deal with the way we live today, in this century.

Don't put your trust in some man and depart from the Lord:

Thus saith the Lord; Cursed be the man that trusteth in man, and maketh flesh his arm, and whose heart departeth from the Lord.

Jeremiah 17:5

We see this happening in our political system. Some good-looking guy runs for office, and we get excited: "Oh, this fellow is going to make some big changes in our country! He's smart, he's compassionate, he's experienced, he's got the big picture!" Then he blows it in some area, and we wonder, *What happened to him?*

That man needs to be relying not on his own good looks, his charisma, or his smarts, but every day of his private and public life, he needs to be on his knees before God asking for divine wisdom and guidance! We shouldn't put our trust in him, and he shouldn't be trusting anyone but God the Father. When we put our trust in a man, we're bringing a curse upon our nation.

Sometimes we see people get married, and they forget about God. I want to say to them, "Hey! You wanted a mate so badly. Now you've got one, and you give up the Lord." Then they put their trust in a person and bring a curse on their marriage. Do you want your marriage to be blessed? Then put God at the center of it.

Can you trust in your work?

Cursed be he that doeth the work of the Lord deceitfully, and cursed be he that keepeth back his sword from blood.

Jeremiah 48:10

If you do God's work in a deceitful way, you can bring a curse upon yourself. That's all too obvious with the "televangelist" scandals that have rocked our nation.

And whatsoever ye do, do it heartily, as to the Lord, and not unto men.

Colossians 3:23

Every kind of job there is, keep in mind that your true Master is not your supervisor or your boss, but your Lord.

If you put your trust in your work, you've got a curse on your situation. Your trust has to be in the blood. Your source is not your paycheck—your source is Jesus Christ.

You can't steal from God and trust in your own money. "Well, I can't afford to tithe," you protest. Do you know what you're really saying? "I trust my money more than I trust God's Word." That will bring a curse:

> **Ye are cursed with a curse: for ye have robbed me.**
>
> **Malachi 3:9**

When you refuse to tithe, you personally bring the curse into your life. But tithing brings blessings.

As we can see, there are many types of family blessings and curses, and God concerns Himself with blessing the four institutions He created: free will, marriage, the family, and nations.

SECTION 3

Jesus Reversed the Curse

11

THE BELIEVER'S COVENANT:
REDEEMED FROM THE CURSE

S in is never fair, but it is predictable. Sins that are repeatedly committed are like weeds planted in the heart. You can mow them down, but until they are understood and dealt with, they will crop back up. Iniquities are like the seeds of weeds—they may die, as your forefathers have, but they will return. Whether the seeds are planted by you, your parents, or your forefathers, the result is a crop of inherited weaknesses or family iniquities:

As the bird by wandering, as the swallow by flying, so the curse causeless shall not come.

Proverbs 26:2

Thou shalt not bow down thyself to them, nor serve them: for I the Lord thy God am a jealous God, visiting the iniquity of the fathers upon the children unto the third and fourth generation of them that hate me.

Exodus 20:5

Remember, the law of iniquity states that the sins of the fathers will continue to the third and fourth generation for those who hate God. But what about those of us who love God? For us, God has made a provision to reverse the curse of iniquities. Just as iniquities are passed through the bloodline, your exemption from the law of iniquity is through blood, the blood sacrifice of your covenant with God. In the old covenant that sacrifice was of bulls and goats, but in the new covenant the perfect, precious blood of Jesus cleanses you from sin and iniquity.

You no longer have to live bound by iniquities and generational curses, being defeated by sin, because Jesus became both your "sin offering" and the "scapegoat" for your iniquities. His physical body was sacrificed and His perfect blood was offered to God for your sins and iniquities. He took your iniquities and buried them in the sea of forgetfulness. You have something better than the "types" and "shadows" of the Old Testament; you have a better covenant in Jesus:

In the same way, after the supper he took the cup, saying, "This cup is the new covenant in my blood, which is poured out for you."

Luke 22:20 NIV

Jesus took on Himself the curse of your iniquity. He became cursed that you could be set free and blessed:

> **Christ hath redeemed us from the curse of the law, being made a curse for us: for it is written, Cursed is every one that hangeth on a tree.**
>
> **Galatians 3:13**

YOUR EMANCIPATION PROCLAMATION

Your "emancipation proclamation," the document of your freedom and deliverance from generational curses and iniquities, is found in Isaiah 53:5,11:

> **But he was wounded for our transgressions, *he was bruised for our iniquities:* the chastisement of our peace was upon him; and with his stripes we are healed. He [God] shall see the travail of his soul, and shall be satisfied: by his knowledge shall my righteous servant [Jesus] justify many; *for he shall bear their iniquities.***

Why was Jesus "bruised" for our iniquities? Because our iniquities, our inherent weaknesses, are like bruises. As we've already seen, natural bruises leave a discoloration. They usually hurt the most when you first get them, then they become discolored. Bruises can go very deep, even to the bone. Bruises of the heart—iniquities—can begin with a crisis such as death, abuse, or trauma that may begin a pattern of sin which is passed on to the next generation. Unlike broken bones that can be set or a wound that can be sown up, bruises can't be treated. A medical doctor will tell you to live with the bruise and it will eventually go away. What the doctor means is that your body will repair itself. Your blood provides nourishment to the body's cells and takes away the waste. Just as your natural blood brings health to areas that are bruised and moves waste, the blood of Jesus is required to heal your heart bruises and carry away your iniquities. Bruises of the heart don't heal by themselves and go away; you must apply the blood of Christ for complete recovery.

> *If you drop an apple, it bruises. In fact, when an apple is bruised, it discolors, begins to rot, and eventually the entire apple spoils.*

Maybe a better example is what happens to a piece of fruit that gets bruised. If you drop an apple, it bruises. In fact, when an apple is bruised, it discolors, it begins to rot, and eventually the entire apple spoils. Without the help of Jesus, the bruises you receive from your iniquities, if not dealt with, will cause your heart to rot and will affect your entire life. Jesus, however, bore your bruises — your iniquities:

The Spirit of the Lord is upon me, because he hath anointed me to preach the gospel to the poor; he hath sent me to heal the brokenhearted, to preach deliverance to the captives, and recovering of sight to the blind, to set at liberty them that are bruised.

Luke 4:18

PHYSICAL AFFLICTIONS AND GENERATIONAL INIQUITIES

Doctors are aware that physical afflictions can be a result of a generational iniquity. When you show signs of certain diseases, they want to know if you have a family history of that disease. Maybe arthritis, diabetes, or heart problems run in your family.

I was only twenty-three years old when the doctor told me: "You have an enlarged heart; there's nothing you can do about it." The doctor's words tore away at my faith. Immediately the devil reminded me that my father had had a heart attack and now the same thing was going to happen to me.

I'm sure that the devil held his breath as he waited to see how I would respond to his lie. I was a young Christian at that time, but I knew enough of God's Word to stand in faith for physical healing. While it is true that my dad did have a heart attack, I knew that Jesus had come to replace family iniquities with blessings and to set me free from every life-threatening sickness.

My husband prayed with me, and we stood on the promises found in Isaiah 53:5 and Psalm 103:3,4:

The chastisement of our peace was upon him;
and with his stripes we are healed.

Isaiah 53:5

[Bless the Lord,] **who forgiveth all thine iniquities; who healeth all thy diseases.**

Psalm 103:3,4

That same year I was miraculously healed of an enlarged heart! Just recently I had my yearly checkup; the doctor said, "Your heart is excellent." God reversed the curse that Satan tried to pass down to me from my father. I have a "fixed" heart. You don't have to live under physical curses because Christ has redeemed you from the curse.

ROOTS OF INIQUITY

The roots of iniquity are pulled up through the blood of Jesus. Isaiah 53 says that Jesus bore our sin; He was wounded for our trespasses and bruised for our iniquities. The blood of Jesus is all sufficient, powerful, and devastating to family iniquities in your bloodline. To be effective, however, the blood of Jesus must be applied to your situation. Positive thinking, psychological counseling—even doing "religious" things like singing in the choir—while good, will not solve the problem. They may provide temporary relief, but only the blood of Jesus is the permanent answer, transforming your curse into a blessing.

The blood of Jesus has purchased your freedom from iniquity, and the witness of the Holy Spirit applies the anointing that breaks the yoke—freeing you of the shackles of your family iniquities:

And it shall come to pass in that day, that his burden shall be taken away from off thy shoulder,

and his yoke from off thy neck, and the yoke shall be destroyed because of the anointing.

Isaiah 10:27

TYPES AND SHADOWS

The Old Testament is full of types and shadows of things to come. To really understand the provisions of the new covenant, we need to understand what God provided for Old Testament believers. He has made a way for His people to have freedom from generational iniquities.

The Jewish ceremony of the Day of Atonement gives us a picture of redemption. Through this ceremony you can see how Jesus purchased your freedom from iniquities. When this ceremony was reenacted in heaven on your behalf, Jesus became your High Priest and blood sacrifice.

Picture with me the most important day of the Jewish year, the tenth day of the seventh month, Tishri—the Day of Atonement. On that day the sins, trespasses, and iniquities of the people were cleansed. On the eve of the Day of Atonement, the people fasted and humbled themselves and repented. The next morning they gathered before the gates of the outer court in solemn assembly.

While the hushed crowd waited outside the temple grounds, inside the high priest, having already selected two goats, seven rams, and a bull, began the ceremony by washing (purifying) himself and dressing in the holy, linen robes of his office. All but one of the animals, a goat, would be sacrificed. The high priest offered blood sacrifices for the *atonement,* which means "reconciliation" of the guilt by divine sacrifice,[1] for the sanctuary, tabernacle, brazen altar, and his fellow priests.

Then he killed the goat of the sin offering for the sins, trespasses, and iniquities of all the people of Israel. The blood from the goat chosen to be the *sin offering* was sprinkled on the mercy seat for the sins the people. (The mercy seat was the place where the presence of God dwelled—the golden center area on the lid of the ark of the covenant cased between the two cherubim.)

The high priest placed both hands upon the head of the remaining goat, the scapegoat, and confessed over it all the sins, transgressions, and iniquities of the people. Then the scapegoat was released into the wilderness. God had accepted the blood of the goat sacrifice as a sin offering, cleansed them of all their sins, and removed their iniquities. Likewise, the blood of Jesus has cleansed you and your family tree of generational iniquities:

> **And the goat shall bear upon him all their iniquities unto a land not inhabited: and he shall let go the goat in the wilderness.**
>
> **Leviticus 16:22**

A HEROINE OF THE OLD COVENANT

I believe on one such Day of Atonement that waiting for cleansing from iniquities with the others was a young woman named Jehosheba. She was the bride of a young priest, and the daughter and granddaughter of two of the most evil and wicked women in the Bible—Jezebel and Athalia.

Jehosheba had possibly the worst family tree of anyone in the Bible; yet God, even in Old Testament times, redeemed her from the iniquities of her family. The book of 1 Kings tells her family history.

Omri, Jehosheba's great-grandfather, was a "bad" king of the Northern Kingdom called Israel. He was a shrewd politician and sought to make peace with the nation of Zidon by marrying his son to Jezebel, who became the wife of Ahab. Jezebel introduced the nation of Israel to the worship of Baal—the most despicable, demonic religion of that day.

The prophet Elijah opposed Ahab and Jezebel and pronounced that there would be a drought in the land. After three years Elijah faced down the prophets of Baal by calling down fire to consume his sacrifice to God. He then called upon the Lord to end the drought. Elijah also prophesied a curse upon Ahab and Jezebel and their descendants. He told them their family would be extinguished.

That was only the beginning of the bad news for Jehosheba. In an attempt to bring peace between the Northern and Southern kingdoms, the "good" king of Judah, Jehoshaphat, accepted a marriage between his son and the daughter of Jezebel, Athalia. Like her mother, Athalia introduced the worship of Baal to her husband and the Southern Kingdom of Judah. After her husband died in battle, his son, Ahaziah, became king. After a few years he was killed.

Athalia saw her son's death as an opportunity to take the throne of Judah and sent assassins to murder her grandchildren. She believed that she could gain the throne of Judah by eliminating all her son's heirs. What a grandmother! She became the only woman to reign in both the Northern and Southern kingdoms. Had she succeeded in killing all of her grandchildren, the seed of David would have ended and there would have been no Messiah because Jesus had to come through the seed of David.

When Jehosheba heard what her mother was doing, she slipped into the nursery and saved the youngest child from the assassin's blade. She and her husband guarded the child until he was seven years old. Then her husband brought him to the temple to be crowned king, and Athalia was killed.

Jehosheba became one of the little-known heroines of the Bible despite her family tree. God doesn't care how rotten your family tree is. When you receive His cleansing, your family iniquities are broken! If God could deliver Jehosheba under the old covenant, just think what He can do through a new and better covenant for you, your children, and the next generation.

> *God doesn't care how rotten your family tree is. When you receive His cleansing, your family iniquities are broken!*

If you are concerned about your family because, unlike Jehosheba, your mate isn't a priest or even a believer yet and you see family iniquities wreaking havoc in your home, then take heart. Remember, it takes only one believing mate to sanctify a house. If you are that one believing person in your home, it's enough. You can end the generational curse and establish the blessing for your family tree, as we already read in 1 Corinthians 7:14.

THE CURSE REVERSED

Before I was saved and Spirit-filled, I attended a Sunday school class, and everything the teacher said, I challenged. It's rather embarrassing now to recall some of the ridiculous things I said back then. I certainly never mentioned them to my daughter, Sarah.

When Sarah was a junior at Oral Roberts University, she spent a summer in Germany at a university. When she returned to the United States, she told me that she wasn't sure that she believed in Jesus. My heart went down to my feet as I listened to her say some of the very things I had said so long ago in that Sunday school class. Sarah was raised in a Spirit-filled home, brought up on the Word of God, and had received the Lord at an early age.

The Lord spoke to me and said, "Don't fall apart—be cool!" So I told her, "The enemy is trying to steal your faith, but Jesus will make Himself real to you." Needless to say, my husband, Wally, and I prayed. After returning to ORU, Sarah called me one night. She had recommitted her life to the Lord. When I asked her how it happened, she told me about a young man at school with whom she was studying. He had experienced a similar loss of faith while studying at Harvard. His father insisted that he attend ORU for a year; and, consequently, he regained the truth of his salvation. This young man, having himself just returned to the Lord, led her back to the truth.

Coincidence? No, God had reversed the curse and had begun the blessing, and He will do the same thing in your life and for your next generation!

┌─────────┐
│ **12** │
└─────────┘

THE REWARDS OF
YOUR REDEMPTION

Man was created with a desire and need for an intimate relationship with God. There is a place in everyone that craves a father–son or father–daughter relationship with his or her Creator. Until that void is filled and the desire satisfied by a relationship with Him, human beings will search for the answer, trying various substitutes to satisfy their desires. Mankind is out of balance and incomplete without a personal relationship with God.

I remember the first time I heard of a child's divorcing his parents. I was aghast at the idea. Yet when Adam and Eve sinned, that was exactly what they did; they divorced their Father, God. Many of us have been deeply wounded by the rejection of a loved one, but that only gives us a small glimmer of how Adam's act of sin and rebellion must have broken the heart of God. How did the One who is defined by the word *love* feel when His children divorced Him through an act of disobedience?

What did God do? Did he become angry, pout, seek vengeance, or hide and nurse His pain? No, out of His great love for you and me, He initiated a plan made before the foundation of the world that would make it possible for all men to return to a relationship of intimacy with Him:

> **For God so loved the world, that he gave his only begotten Son, that whosoever believeth in him should not perish, but have everlasting life.**
>
> **John 3:16**

Not only did man lose his relationship with God, but he brought upon himself and this world the curse of sin and sin's companion, death. When Adam and Eve chose rebellion over obedience and sin over righteousness, they "adopted" a new father and god—Satan. They poisoned themselves and all creation with their sin. God withdrew from intimacy with man because in His goodness, God is repulsed by sin and he must judge it. Adam and Eve had made themselves an enemy of God. Sin is more than an obnoxious irritant to God; it is His enemy:

> **Wherefore, as by one man sin entered into the world, and death by sin; and so death passed upon all men, for that all have sinned.**
>
> **Romans 5:12**

Satan must have been filled with malicious glee over his part in the corruption of man. I'm sure he felt that he had won a major battle with God, because the very creatures whom God had lovingly crafted were now in the camp of the enemy. Did Satan win that day? No way:

> **He that committeth sin is of the devil; for the devil sinneth from the beginning. For this purpose the Son of God was manifested, that he might destroy the works of the devil.**
>
> **1 John 3:8**

Jesus stripped himself of His glory and humbled Himself to be born as a man for the dual purpose of destroying the works of the devil in your life and restoring you to sonship with the Father. Why salvation? So you can end the curse of sin and iniquity in your life and your family's life and establish generational blessings:

> **For sin shall not have dominion over you...ye were the servants of sin, but ye have obeyed from the heart....Being then made free from sin ye became the servants of righteousness.... For the wages of sin is death; but the gift of God is eternal life through Jesus Christ our Lord.**
>
> **Romans 6:14,17,18,23**

The thief cometh not, but for to steal, and to kill, and to destroy: *I am come that they might have life, and that they might have it more abundantly.*

John 10:10

OLD THINGS PASSED AWAY

I think one of the saddest stories in the Bible is that of Judas, a man who remained bound by the iniquity of greed while in the presence of the One who could release him. This greed caused him to betray Jesus, the Son of God. In Acts 1:18 it says:

Now this man [Judas] purchased a field with the reward of iniquity; and falling headlong, he burst asunder in the midst, and all his bowels gushed out.

Judas carried the moneybag because he was the treasurer of Jesus' ministry team. It's hard to imagine how someone could walk with, talk with, see miracles performed by, and be with Jesus for over three years and still be bound by a family curse or an iniquity of his own making. Judas illustrates that being a "hearer of the Word" is not enough. To enter into the rewards of your redemption, you have to become a "doer" also:

Do not merely listen to the word, and so deceive yourselves. Do what it says. Anyone who listens to the word but does not do what it says is like a man who looks at his face in a mirror and, after looking at

himself, goes away and immediately forgets what he looks like.

James 1:22-24 NIV

One legacy of your former life is the curse of sin that all mankind received through Adam and Eve's act of disobedience. That state of sinfulness was judged by God, and mankind merely awaited the execution of the sentence. Jesus took that sentence and bore the penalty of sin for you, me, and all mankind. He died in our place:

For as by one man's [Adam's] **disobedience many were made sinners, so by the obedience of one** [Jesus] **shall many be made righteous.**

Romans 5:19

You were delivered from your sin nature. As a sinner, sin was natural for you, but when you made Jesus the Lord of your life, your sin nature passed away, and you became new in Christ and now have His nature in you:

Therefore if any man be in Christ, he is a new creature: *old things are passed away;* **behold, all things are become new.**

2 Corinthians 5:17

The domination and the power of the sin nature was defeated in your life. Where before you were obligated to sin, you now have a choice and a desire not to sin. You are free of sin's authority to live a victorious life that pleases God. Yes, it's still possible to hear the voice and give in to the temptation of sin, but sin will never be able to regain control over you. You are free:

> **Knowing this, that our old man is crucified with him** [Christ]**, that the body of sin might be destroyed, that henceforth we should not serve sin.... For sin shall not have dominion over you.**
>
> **Romans 6:6,14**

ALL THINGS BECOME NEW

In previous chapters we discussed that family iniquities can come in the forms of anger, obesity, alcoholism, and so forth. These iniquities are the obstinate sins, and recurring family illnesses are passed on through the bloodline. There is no question that Jesus, acting as your sin sacrifice and the scapegoat for iniquities, dealt the death-blow to this problem area:

> **Who gave himself for us, that he might redeem us from all iniquity, and purify unto himself a peculiar people, zealous of good works.**
>
> **Titus 2:14**

Many Christians suffer from a personality crisis. They know *what* they are—new creatures in Christ—but they don't know *who* they are and how their new identity relates to their victory over family iniquities:

**I am crucified with Christ: nevertheless I live;
yet not I, but Christ liveth in me: and the life which I
now live in the flesh I live by the faith of the Son of
God, who loved me, and gave himself for me.**

Galatians 2:20

You are a new creature in Christ! According to the Greek
translation of 2 Corinthians 5:17, God created you as a "new
being who has never existed before." That means those hereditary
family iniquities are no longer your heritage. You've heard the
expression, "That's just not you." Those family iniquities just
aren't you anymore! You have a new birthright. As a child of
God, you have a wonderful inheritance: blessings instead of
curses, abundance instead of lack, and health instead of
sickness:

**Giving thanks to the Father, who has qualified
you to share in the inheritance of the saints in the
kingdom of light. For he has rescued us from the
dominion of darkness and brought us into the
kingdom of the Son he loves, in whom we have
redemption, the forgiveness of sins.**

Colossians 1:12-14 NIV

You once were an enemy of God, but now He sees you as a
child, a new person re-created in the likeness of Himself. When
proud parents show off their newborn baby, people say things
like: "He has his father's eyes, his mother's chin," and so forth.
When God looks at you, He says: "Yes, he has My
righteousness and My love, and he looks just like My Son."

Every time you find the words *in Christ* in the New Testament, give them special attention because they describe what you look like to God. Hold those Scriptures before you like a mirror—they are the real you:

> **When we were God's enemies, we were reconciled to him through the death of his Son.**
>
> **Romans 5:10 NIV**

> **Because those who are led by the Spirit of God are sons of God.... You received the Spirit of sonship. And by him we cry, "Abba, Father."**
>
> **Romans 8:14,15 NIV**

Jesus sees you as an individual member of the body of Christ. Under His leadership, you are more than a conqueror, victoriously overcoming every strategy of the enemy in your life. You are a citizen of His kingdom with kingdom rights and responsibilities: you have eternal life, victory over sin and Satan, the right to use the name of Jesus in prayer, the right to the indwelling of the Holy Spirit, and more:

> **No, in all these things we are more than conquerors through him who loved us.**
>
> **Romans 8:37 NIV**

> **Now you are the body of Christ, and each one of you is a part of it.**
>
> **1 Corinthians 12:27 NIV**

GOD'S POWER IN YOU

Have you tried and tried and yet failed to overcome your hereditary weaknesses? Then you are close to deliverance. If you have discovered that your own efforts will never be enough to secure a lasting victory, then you are ready to turn to God's power to destroy the ties—your inherent weaknesses—that bind you:

> **But as many as receive him, to them gave he** *power to become the sons of God,* **even to them that believe on his name.**

> **John 1:12**

When you were born again, God came to live in you to restore you to the wholeness of "sonship." Having lived for years as a slave to family iniquities, you defined yourself by your weaknesses. You may have heard yourself saying things like: "I'm always sick; I go from one thing to another! I'll always be poor too. Why, if it weren't for bad luck, I'd have no luck at all! I've tried to give up drinking, but it's stronger than I am. I'll go to my grave doing it—just like my dad did."

You can define yourself down to being a powerless creature—a victim of your own weaknesses. But you are not a victim but a victor; not a loser but a winner; not on the bottom but above every sin, situation, and sickness.

You don't have to plead and beg for deliverance; the gift has already been given to you. You don't have to be worthy, go to Bible school, be called to full-time ministry, or be perfect with no past mistakes. This very minute you have within you the power of God.

This power is not just for your salvation—that was only the beginning. As a child of God, you are promised an abundant life:

I am come that they might have life, and that they might have it more abundantly.

John 10:10

God's power will roll over and crash through anything—including family iniquities—that stand between you and the abundant life due to you as a child of God. It is time for you to redefine yourself by the Scriptures and assume your real identity as God's son or daughter—a supernatural being who wields the power to break the curse in your family tree and to establish generational blessings.

RECEIVE REDEMPTION

Your redemption from sin, trespasses, and iniquities was purchased once and for all by Jesus Christ through His death, burial, and resurrection. Jesus forged a new covenant with His shed blood to free mankind from sin and death:

Whosoever shall call on the name of the Lord shall be saved.

Acts 2:21

Have you accepted Jesus as Lord and Savior? Have you joined the family of God? Only those who are born again can be free from generational iniquities—the negative spiritual traits that you have either begun or those passed on to you by your forefathers. Your only escape is to be born anew through the blood of Jesus and to receive God, our spiritual Father. When you become born again, your old family traits are canceled and the qualities and blessings of Jesus become your birthright:

For whom he did foreknow, he also did predestinate *to be conformed to the image of his Son, that he might be the firstborn among many brethren.*

Romans 8:29

Perhaps you have never received the new birth, or maybe you have grown cold in your relationship with God. Maybe family iniquities have caused you to give up and backslide:

And because iniquity shall abound, the love of many shall wax cold.

Matthew 24:12

You can change that now. If you are sincere and want to find freedom from your family iniquities, and if you desire a fresh new start, pray this prayer out loud:

Dear Jesus, I believe that You died for my sins, transgressions, and iniquities and that You rose again on the third day. I confess to You that I am a sinner and that I need Your love and forgiveness. Come into my life, forgive my sins, and give me eternal life. I confess You now as my Lord. Thank You for my salvation! Amen.

Congratulations! Your acceptance of Jesus Christ as your Lord and Savior is the best decision that you have ever made. You have become a new creation in Christ. The Trinity dwells in you: God the Father, Jesus the Son, and the Holy Spirit. You are set free from sin and servitude to Satan:

> **Therefore if any man be in Christ, he is a new creature.**
>
> **2 Corinthians 5:17**

> **For the law of the Spirit of life in Christ Jesus hath made me free from the law of sin and death.**
>
> **Romans 8:2**

Welcome to God's family! Welcome to His life!

$$\boxed{13}$$

BREAKING THE PATTERN
ONCE AND FOR ALL

Not long ago we had the bushes trimmed in front of our home. Some of them were overgrown and really looked bad, so we had a man come and trim them back to stumps. We thought the man who trimmed the bushes would pick up the trimmings and haul them to the dump. However, he left them and didn't come back. So we called and left messages on his answering machine. Finally, he came back with his truck, and I thought, *Good, the problem is solved*. However, he didn't put the limbs and rubbish in his truck; he bound them into bundles and placed them by the curb. He said, "The trash men will pick them up." There were five or six large bundles over six feet high. I thought, *The trash haulers will take one look at all this and say, "Forget that!"*

The next morning was our day for trash pick-up, so when I left my home for work I prayed, "Lord, surround my trash with favor." When I returned home, I was so relieved to see all those bundles gone. I thought, *Thank You, Lord!* Then the Lord spoke to me and said, *Marilyn, the garbage in a person's life can't be surrounded with favor; neither can I be expected to carry it off. I can't give favor to garbage or cover it over. The way to get rid of trash is by repenting of it. Then the blood of Jesus cleanses, and past sins are cast into the sea of forgetfulness.*

God wants you to get rid of the trash in your life. He will not overlook it or give it favor. He wants you to take the steps necessary to deal with family iniquities in your life.

Acknowledge and Confess the Iniquities of Your Forefathers

In chapter 4 you uncovered the roots of the iniquities in your family tree. You asked yourself, "What sins, habits, failures, or illnesses do I know of in the lives of my forefathers?" You dealt with each person in your last four or five generations individually, starting with your father and mother.

Now put your list of family iniquities before the Lord and get His cleansing. The blood of Jesus will cleanse your bloodline, and God will release His power to deliver your family tree from generational iniquities.

FORGIVE YOUR FAMILY INIQUITIES

You may not feel very forgiving toward your forefathers because their iniquities have caused you such problems. You must guard against the "victim" attitude, however. You aren't a victim in Christ Jesus; you're a victor. Your forefathers may have passed along to you a weakness for the enemy to use against you, but you make the choice to act on it or break it. To break the cycle of iniquity for yourself and the next generation, you must forgive your forefathers:

> **Forgive us our debts, as we also have forgiven our debtors. For if you forgive men when they sin against you, your heavenly Father will also forgive you.**
>
> **Matthew 6:12,14 NIV**

Many people have been terribly hurt by their parents or other family members. Perhaps you are one of those people and feel you have a right never to speak to them again. However, if you don't forgive them, you will judge them and your judgment will return to haunt you. Romans 2:1 says that whatever you judge others for, you are guilty of doing yourself. Your judging can set up a new family iniquity for you and your children:

> **Therefore thou art inexcusable, O man, whosoever thou art that judgest: for wherein thou judgest another, thou condemnest thyself; *for thou that judgest doest the same things.***

ASK GOD TO FORGIVE SPECIFIC
SINS OF LIVING FOREFATHERS

Forgiving others so that you will be forgiven is very important. You cannot get total freedom from your family iniquities or any painful situation inflicted on you by another until you release them from their transgressions. Forgiving is not denying the sin or trespasses against you, nor denying that you suffered pain because of their actions; nor does forgiving deny the personal cost of another's actions. Choosing to walk in or live a lifestyle of forgiveness is very calculated. After counting the cost of others' sins against you—the unpaid debt that transgression has created in your life—you make the decision to cancel their debt when you forgive them. That is how God forgives you. He doesn't ignore your sins or cover them up. Rather, He looks to the blood of Jesus and stamps your debt "paid in full." By His grace and with His help you can do the same. Here are biblical examples of how to do so.

Then said Jesus, Father forgive them; for they know not what they do.

Luke 23:34

And he [Stephen] kneeled down, and cried with a loud voice, Lord, lay not this sin to their charge. And when he had said this, he fell asleep.

Acts 7:60

Confess Your Participation in the Iniquities of Your Forefathers

Don't brush lightly over this step in the process to gain your freedom from family iniquities. We have a tendency to avoid taking blame. There used to be a comedian who excused every mistake he made with the phrase, "The devil made me do it." In light of your new understanding of family iniquities, you must be careful and not excuse your own sins by thinking, *My forefathers made me do that*. Your forefathers provided you with the spiritual weakness, and the devil has no doubt taken advantage of your vulnerability. But never for a moment forget that you—by your free will—commit the sin. You are accountable.

Remember, God will not cover up your trash, overlook your sin, or excuse it because it is a family weakness. God expects you to repent. The consequences for not dealing with sin as a Christian are grave. Unconfessed sin is the mountain made from a molehill, because by not dealing with sin you give place to the devil in your life—you give him a stronghold, a high place, a place of authority from which to operate:

He that covereth his sins shall not prosper: but whoso confesseth and forsaketh them shall have mercy.

Proverbs 28:13

Neither give place to the devil.

Ephesians 4:27

The consequences of not confessing your sins are terrible, but the rewards for taking responsibility and facing God with them are wonderful. God will give you mercy, forgiveness, and cleansing from all unrighteousness. The God of love loved you before you were born again and loves you just as much now. It doesn't matter how grievous your sin or how badly you feel you have blown it and disappointed Him. God is like the father of the prodigal son, waiting with open arms to hug you, clasp you to Himself, and return you to your rightful place in His kingdom. (Luke 15:11-32.) Like the prodigal son, you may be dirty and smelly from wallowing with the pigs, but God doesn't care about your "hygiene"; He'll clean you up. He wants you to come home:

> **But where sin abounded, grace did much more abound.**
>
> **Romans 5:20**

ASK GOD TO FORGIVE AND CLEANSE YOU

Now that you have confessed—accepted the responsibility for—your sin, ask God to forgive and cleanse you, and He will:

> **But if we walk in the light, as he is in the light, we have fellowship one with another, and the blood of Jesus Christ his Son cleanseth us from all sin. If we say that we have no sin, we deceive ourselves, and the truth is not in us. If we confess our sins, he is faithful and just to forgive us our sins, and to cleanse us from all unrighteousness.**
>
> **1 John 1:7-9**

Now pray this prayer with me:

Father, I thank You for Your Word which is a lamp unto my feet and a light unto my path. I thank You for redemption through the blood of Jesus. I give myself to You. I ask You to cleanse me from all sin and iniquity. Forgive us—myself, my parents, and my forefathers—of all unrighteousness. Cleanse me now by the blood from all sins, diseases, infirmities, and attitudes that are not like You. I believe that You are breaking the link of iniquity and delivering me, my children, and the next generation from the bondage of hereditary weaknesses. In Jesus' name. Amen!

SUBMIT YOUR WILL TO GOD

Each step we have covered is important, but this next step is what will lock in your freedom from bondage and permanently put family iniquities in your past. The key is to submit. Adam's sin was one of rebellion against God, and the opposite of rebellion is submission. Jesus submitted to the Father, and so must we. Submission is not being God's robot but rather choosing to accept God's plan for your life. It is saying: "You are the Creator, and I'm the creation. I accept Your lordship over me. Your plan is better than my plan, and I want to do things Your way." God is this moment at work in the area of your will because it is vital to the completion of your victory:

BREAKING GENERATIONAL CURSES

**Continue to work out your salvation with fear
and trembling, for it is God who works in you to will
and to act according to his good purpose.**

Philippians 2:12,13 NIV

God cannot supernaturally empower your unsubmitted will.
Until your will is in agreement with His will, you are operating
under your own power. It isn't God's purpose to *break* your will;
He wants you to end your rebellion so you can find your victory.
God's order for your victory is submit to Him and resist the
devil. Once you have submitted, you are enabled to successfully
resist the devil:

Submit yourselves, then, to God. *Resist the devil,
and he will flee from you.*

James 4:7 NIV

Jesus Suffered the Curse and Overcame the Devil for You

Have you suffered enough yet? Some people feel they must
suffer the guilt and shame of their sins themselves. Stop it! You
insult the work of Christ on the cross by continuing to live in
guilt and shame for your past sins and iniquities:

**Christ hath redeemed us from the curse of the
law, being made a curse for us: for it is written,
Cursed is every one that hangeth on a tree: that the
blessing of Abraham might come on the Gentiles,**

through Jesus Christ; that we might receive the promise of the Spirit through faith.

Galatians 3:13,14

Who gave himself for us, that he might redeem us from all iniquity, and purify unto himself a peculiar people, zealous of good works.

Titus 2:14

You are the righteousness of God through the blood of Jesus. God sees you not as guilty but as righteous. God is not ashamed of you; He is proud of you. You did not earn this position with God by any good deeds or by acts of penitence. It's part of the package of salvation. It is time to bring your self-image in line with God's view of you:

For he hath made him to be sin for us, who knew no sin; that we might be made the righteousness of God in him.

2 Corinthians 5:21

God's Word says that you are healed not only of your diseases but of the shame and guilt of your sins, iniquities, and trespasses. Receive by faith a healing in your thought patterns:

But he was wounded for our transgressions, he was bruised for our iniquities: the chastisement of our peace was upon him; and with his stripes we are healed.

Isaiah 53:5

Remember from an earlier chapter that we discussed Satan's victory when Adam sinned. Satan believed that he had won. Man was a casualty of the conflict, but the devil didn't care. God, however, cares about you! God loves people! He sent Jesus to take the punishment for your sin and reverse the curse of your family iniquities:

> **For this purpose the Son of God was manifested, that he might destroy the works of the Devil** [in your life].
>
> **1 John 3:8**

GOD HAS ALL AUTHORITY

You need to understand your line of authority. Do you have authority? What is it? How does it work? Why should God give it to you?

God is the source for all authority and power. He is King of kings and Lord of lords. A proud King Nebuchadnezzar learned this lesson the hard way but finally looked up to heaven and said:

> **He** [God] **doeth according to his will in the army of heaven, and among the inhabitants of the earth: and none can stay his hand, or say unto him, What doest thou?**
>
> **Daniel 4:35**

God delegated His authority to Jesus. Let's pull back the curtain and watch the passing of the scepter of power through the eyes of Daniel:

> **In my vision at night I looked, and there before me was one like a son of man [Jesus], coming with the clouds of heaven. He approached the Ancient of Days [God] and was led into his presence. He was given authority, glory and sovereign power; all peoples, nations and men of every language worshiped him. His dominion is an everlasting dominion that will not pass away, and his kingdom is one that will never be destroyed.**
>
> **Daniel 7:13** NIV

Jesus delegated His authority to believers. You can't earn it. You don't deserve it in your own right; nevertheless, Jesus *gave* you the gift of authority. Take the scepter of His authority and use it to be set free from your family iniquities:

> **"I have given you *authority* to trample on snakes and scorpions and *to overcome all the power of the enemy;* nothing will harm you."**
>
> **Luke 10:19** NIV

USE THE AUTHORITY OF THE NAME OF JESUS

Don't allow the commonality of the name of Jesus to cause you to forget the raw power of that name. *Jesus* is the name above every name. Devils quiver at that name, angels launch into flight at that name, the sick are healed by the power of the name of Jesus. No evil thing can stand against the name of Jesus. At the name of Jesus your family iniquities have no choice but to bow:

> *"In my name* **they will drive out demons; they will speak in new tongues; they will pick up snakes with their hands; and when they drink deadly poison, it will not hurt them at all; they will place their hands on sick people, and they will get well."**
>
> **Mark 16:17,18** NIV

> **"I tell you the truth, my Father will give you whatever you ask in my name. Until now you have not asked for anything** *in my name.* **Ask and you will receive, and your joy will be complete."**
>
> **John 16:23,24** NIV

Why did Jesus give you power through His name? To bring glory to God. When you become set free from your family iniquities—the strongholds and high places of the enemy in your life, in the lives of your children and the next generation—think of the pleasure that victory brings to God. The devil may have had the first laugh when he seduced Adam and Eve to sin, but God has the last laugh when the hold of sin and Satan is broken off your life:

> **And I will do whatever you ask** *in my name,* **so that the Son may bring glory to the Father. You may ask me for anything** *in my name,* **and I will do it.**
>
> **John 14:13,14** NIV

Declare the Power of the Blood of Jesus

Without the precious blood of Jesus, all the preceding steps of deliverance are as nothing. It is His blood that cleanses you from sin and iniquity, reconciles you to the Father, gives you the victory over death and the grave and makes all things possible. The steps to your victory over family iniquities begin and end at the Cross and with the shed blood of Christ. Satan was completely fooled; he thought you were sentenced without parole—no pardon was possible. But God loved you so much He sent Jesus to die for your freedom:

> **Jesus replied, I tell you the truth, everyone who sins is a slave to sin. Now a slave has no permanent place in the family, but a son belongs to it forever.** *So if the Son sets you free, you will be free indeed.*
>
> **John 8:34-36** NIV

> **In fact, the law requires that nearly everything be cleansed with blood, and without the shedding of blood there is no forgiveness.**
>
> **Hebrews 9:22** NIV

Declare That Your Curses Are Broken

It is time for you to make a faith declaration concerning your family iniquities. You are full of God's Word, and the Word has built your faith. Declare boldly, using your God-given authority, your total victory over every family iniquity. Name each and every thing that has caused you to be less than a victor. Call both heaven and hell to witness your emancipation proclamation. Your faith-filled testimony is the final straw to break the devil's back:

> **And they overcame him by the blood of the Lamb,** *and by the word of their testimony;* **and they loved not their lives unto the death.**
>
> **Revelation 12:11**

Your faith-filled words are the match that ignites the dynamite that will explode the family iniquities from your life. God's power and authority in you are like a coiled spring waiting for release. It is only potential power until you release it with words into your area of need:

> **Have faith in God. For verily I say unto you, That whosoever shall say unto this mountain, Be thou removed, and be thou cast into the sea; and shall not doubt in his heart, but shall believe that those things which he saith shall come to pass; he shall have whatsoever he saith.**
>
> **Mark 11:22,23**

Your words have authority both in heaven and on earth. Your mouth has the power to bind the works of Satan—family iniquities—and to loose the blessings of God in your life:

Whatsoever ye shall bind on earth shall be bound in heaven: and whatsoever ye shall loose on earth shall be loosed in heaven.

Matthew 18:18

What you speak to yourself about yourself is also vitally important. Did you know that you have already died and been buried? It's true. When you received salvation you were identified with Jesus' death and resurrection. Begin saying to yourself, "I am dead to sin and alive unto God."

Knowing this, that our old man is crucified with him, that the body of sin might be destroyed, that henceforth we should not serve sin.

Romans 6:6

Likewise reckon ye also yourselves to be dead indeed unto sin, but alive unto God through Jesus Christ our Lord.

Romans 6:11

SPEAK BLESSINGS OVER YOUR LIFE AND THE LIVES OF YOUR CHILDREN

What you say about yourself and your family is more important than what others say about you. Your words have power. You can bless or curse yourself and your family by what you say. By speaking the blessings from God's Word, you release God's best into your situation. You have a heritage of blessing from your heavenly Father; speak it over yourself and your children:

> **Christ hath redeemed us from the curse...that the blessing of Abraham might come on the Gentiles through Jesus Christ.**
>
> **Galatians 3:13,14**

> **Praise be to the God and Father of our Lord Jesus Christ, who has blessed us in the heavenly realms with every spiritual blessing in Christ.**
>
> **Ephesians 1:3** NIV

Now live as though the curse of your family iniquities is defeated and has been replaced with the blessings of God, because it's true. Your fresh start, your new day has come!

STEPS TO BREAKING THE PATTERNS

In chapter 4 we uncovered the root system of your family tree. The following are the steps included in this chapter to help you break the pattern of generational iniquities in your life once and for all. Write down your response to each step so that you may refer to it from time to time. Don't rush; take as long as each step requires. Refer to the questions you answered in chapter 4 in order to fill in the first step.

First step: Allow the Holy Spirit to bring to your remembrance the sins and iniquities of your parents and forefathers, and confess them.

Write the names of each of your forefathers as far back as you can remember. (If you don't know their names, write their relationship to you; i.e., great-grandfather, great-grandmother.)

_____

_____

_____

_____

_____

_____

_____

As you meditate on each person, write down the iniquities in which they were involved. Take the time necessary to be as thorough as possible.

_____

_____

_____

_____

_____

_____

_____

Confess, as if they were your own, your forefathers' iniquities.

Second Step: Personally forgive your forefathers of their iniquities.

Look at your list, and starting with the most distant of your deceased forefathers, ask God to forgive each of his iniquities. Continue until you have gone through each person.

Third Step: Ask God to forgive specific sins of your living forefathers.

Review the iniquities of your living parents and grandparents.

Make a faith decision to forgive—to cancel their debt—those who have wounded you by their sins and iniquities.

Fourth Step: Confess your participation in the iniquities of your family tree.

Accept the responsibility for your own iniquities.

Avoid creating a stronghold for the devil by confessing your participation in your forefathers' iniquities to God.

Fifth Step: Ask God to forgive and cleanse you.

Having accepted responsibility and confessed your participation in family iniquities, ask forgiveness.

Sixth Step: Submit your will to God.

Submit to God's plan for your life to lock in your victory.

Know that your submitted will is supernaturally empowered to make you an overcomer.

Seventh Step: Remember that Jesus suffered the curse and overcame the devil for you.

Understand that you don't have to carry your shame; Jesus bore it.

Allow God to heal and transform a sin-consciousness into righteousness-consciousness.

Eighth Step: Understand that God has all authority.

God has all authority and has delegated it to Jesus.

Jesus has delegated His authority to every born-again believer and has empowered you to be free of family iniquities and all the works of the devil.

Ninth Step: Use the authority of the name of Jesus.

Apply the name *Jesus* to your family iniquities; at the name of Jesus, everything that is named must come under His authority and the authority of the believer who uses His name. (Phil. 2:10.)

Tenth Step: Declare the power of the blood of Jesus.

Jesus purchased your freedom from every family iniquity by his shed blood. Make this your continual confession.

Eleventh Step: Declare that your family's generational curses are broken.

Using your list of family iniquities, name each iniquity and speak faith-filled words to proclaim your victory over each one.

Release the power of God into each situation by your words—the blood of Jesus and your testimony will overcome the devil. (Rev. 12:11.)

Use your authority to bind the work of the enemy and loose the blessings of God into your life and the lives of your children.

Speak only God's truth about your family iniquities; you are dead to sin and alive to God.

Twelfth Step: Speak blessings over your life and the lives of your children.

Be careful to speak *only* blessings (what the Bible says about you) over yourself and your family, because your words have the power to bless or to curse.

14

FREE INDEED!

If the Son therefore shall make you free, ye shall be free indeed.

John 8:36

In the previous chapter, we covered the various steps necessary for breaking the generational curse and establishing a heritage of blessings.

When you were born again, your family iniquities were not just broken; they were reversed, and God blessed you in the areas that used to be cursed. Now you are free indeed! It's not that you'll never have to contend with the iniquities of the past again, but you have taken an important step in reversing your family's curse. In the area in which you were weak, you are now strong. You have set the course for your family's future, and you can begin by faith to walk in generational blessings.

ABUNDANT LIFE

The Word of God promises you an abundant life. The iniquities that you and your family have labored under for so many years did not actually belong to you. Exodus 20:5 says that the sins of the forefathers are passed down to the third and fourth generations of those who hate God. If you are born again, you can rest assured that the love of God has been poured out in your heart by the Holy Spirit and you don't meet the qualifications for a generational curse. (Rom. 5:5.) Those who love Him, He blesses unto a thousand generations.

You might ask, "Well, if I'm born again and Jesus has blessed the areas of my life that used to be cursed, why didn't those iniquities cease to operate in my life?" Because the areas were never dealt with. For the most part, Christians come against the symptoms and not the root cause of a problem. For example, if your child misbehaves in school, you would probably focus on the misbehavior instead of searching out the root cause, which could be a classroom bully or a verbally abusive teacher. Likewise, unless you know what the Bible says about you and your inheritance in Christ, the devil will continue to bully you *even after salvation*, killing, stealing from, and destroying you and the future members of your family tree.

SANCTIFICATION OF THE SOUL

At the time of your born-again experience, there was no question that you received a new spirit and a new nature. You received the incorruptible seed, Jesus Christ, who sanctified you and set you apart for the Master's use. The real you, your recreated spirit, no longer wanted to sin against God. Although the inward man may have desired to refrain from past sins, I'm sure that many of you will admit to still blowing it from time to time because of the mystery of iniquity still at work in your old nature. Why? Because *parts* of you were surrendered to the lordship of Jesus Christ and not your entire being.

The word *sanctification* means "to make holy, consecrate, to set apart."[1] Many in the body of Christ are aware of the sanctifying work that takes place in their spirits at the time of salvation, but few seem to understand that this process must also take place in their souls, where the mind, will, and emotions reside:

> **And may the God of peace Himself sanctify you through and through—that is, separate you from profane things, make you pure and wholly consecrated to God—and may your spirit and soul and body be preserved sound and complete [and found] blameless at the coming of our Lord Jesus Christ.**
>
> **1 Thessalonians 5:23 AMP**

Until your soul is sanctified or set apart and holy unto the Lord, a door is left open for the bruises of family iniquities to continue to harm you and your future generations. We've all heard horror stories about upstanding Christian men and women who led exemplary lives but were closet alcoholics or who molested their children.

Sin begins in the soul; therefore, sanctification must take place there also. A person who is caught stealing didn't just wake up one day and decide to become a thief. No, he entertained the idea in his mind long before he decided to act upon it.

One of the best ways I have found to sanctify the soul is through reading the Word of God, which washes your mind, will, and emotions from everything that could hinder the will of God. Daily Bible reading can cleanse your soul of the evil seeds that could defile it. You may think it is all right for you to become angry, hold bitterness in your heart, or nurse a grudge; however, 1 Thessalonians 5:23 says your whole spirit, soul, and body must be sanctified. James also bears witness to this truth:

> **From whence come wars and fightings among you? come they not hence, even of your lusts that war in your members?**
>
> **James 4:1**

Sanctification of the soul is a process. Consequently, you may have surrendered parts of your being (your spirit and perhaps your body) to the lordship of Jesus Christ, but the *whole* man must be sanctified or set apart for the Master's use. One of the purposes of breaking the pattern of generational iniquities is to allow this sanctifying process to take place so that you will have complete and total freedom in Christ in every area of your life.

THE BLESSINGS OF ABRAHAM

And I will bless them that bless thee, and curse him that curseth thee.

Genesis 12:3

Your family blessings are guaranteed. Abraham received the blessings of God by faith. When Balaam was summoned to curse the Israelites, he could not because they had been blessed in Abraham's loins. The king of Moab became angry with Balaam and said, "Why don't you curse these people? I've told you to curse them, and you keep blessing them!" Balaam answered, "You just can't curse what God has blessed." (Num. 23:8.)

The same principle holds true for you and your family tree. You have come into the knowledge of the truth of God's Word about generational blessings, and you will never be satisfied by accepting anything less than His best. You now know that you will never again have to put up with the devil's junk. If symptoms resurface of something that has been reversed, you can stand your ground and speak God's

> *You have come into the knowledge of the truth of God's Word about generational blessings, and you will never be satisfied by accepting anything less than His best.*

Word to that area of your life. You can tell the devil that
Galatians 3:13 says you've been redeemed from the curse and
only blessings can be inherited by your family tree.

One mistake many Christians make is thinking they can
defeat the devil once and for all. No, the devil may come at you
with the same generational weaknesses time and time again. Just
remind him of the Word of God, and declare your freedom!

THE WOUNDS OF A TRESPASS

A sanctified soul is one that is healed and whole in Christ
Jesus, and the wounds of a trespass cannot enter. The mind, will,
and emotions have been cleansed of past hurts and iniquities,
and they are free to submit to the lordship of Jesus Christ.

Wounds from a trespass adversely impact the mind, will, and
emotions and cut right to the core of a person. Unlike a natural
wound that scabs over and eventually heals, soulish wounds can
only be healed by the blood of Jesus. Otherwise, they will fester
and spread like cancer.

Wounds to the soul are caused by trespasses. We learned that
to trespass means to overstep preestablished boundaries.[2] To
trespass also implies the violation of another person's being.

There are many types of trespasses. You can trespass against
someone verbally by the words you speak to or about them or by
committing acts of violence against them. Everyone has
experienced the wound of a trespass, and either intentionally or
unintentionally, we have all trespassed against others.

To trespass also means to wound or mar. When you trespass against someone and wound them (or vice versa), you literally mar them, or leave a mark or bruise on them, that hurts so badly and penetrates so deeply, they'll remember it for the rest of their lives.

Proverbs 18:8 says, "The words of a talebearer are as wounds, and they go down into the innermost parts of the belly." From this Scripture we can deduce that the old saying, "Sticks and stones may break my bones, but words will never hurt me," is just another lie of the devil. A verbal trespass is a lethal thing.

In 2 Corinthians 12:7, the apostle Paul talks about a thorn in the flesh that was a messenger of Satan sent to buffet him. You can well believe that the trespasses that have been committed against you are thorns or messengers of Satan sent to vex you and thwart the will of God for your life and your future generations.

If you are carrying wounds from trespasses committed against you or that you have committed against others, this is your opportunity to release the guilt and pain and to be set free! Although Jesus set you free from sin at the time of the new birth, many Christians will continue to hold onto the wounds caused by trespasses so they can nurse them. They'll suppress the hurt until something happens that triggers the

> *If you are carrying wounds from trespasses committed against you or that you have committed against others, this is your opportunity to release the guilt and pain and to be set free!*

memory of the pain. Then they'll relive the experience all over again. Although some people find comfort in this, holding onto these trespasses is the root of bitterness, which the writer of Hebrews says will spring up and defile you. (Heb. 12:15.) The blood of Jesus is powerful enough to cleanse you from sins and trespasses.

FAMILY TRESPASSES

Trespasses hurt people and can also destroy family relationships. They are very serious offenses to God. Like sin, transgression, and iniquity, trespassing began in the Garden of Eden with Adam and Eve. After they transgressed against God by eating of the fruit of the tree, the mystery of iniquity was set in motion and passed down to their future generations. In Genesis 4, their son Cain began a family iniquity when he murdered his brother, Abel. This was a trespass, and Abel's blood cried out from the earth for vengeance.

In Genesis 31:36, Jacob was angry with his uncle, Laban, and demanded to know: "What is my trespass?" Jacob knew firsthand what a trespass was because he had trespassed against his brother, Esau, on many occasions. He met his match, however, when he met Laban, who trespassed against Jacob at every available opportunity. Not only did Laban exact seven years labor from Jacob and then give him the wrong wife, he also made him work another seven years for the wife he'd initially promised — and he changed Jacob's wages ten times.

After the wrestling match with the angel and his subsequent name change, Jacob, now called Israel, commanded his son Joseph to forgive his brothers for the trespasses they had committed against him. If you'll recall, Joseph's brothers despised him because their father favored him and also because they recognized the call of God on his life. They stole the many-colored coat his father had made just for him, threw Joseph into a pit, threatened to kill him, sold him as a slave to the Midianites, and lied to their father about what had happened to him. (Gen. 37.)

Although his brothers' actions could have severely wounded Joseph, he chose to forgive them. He understood that what had happened to him was a part of God's plan to make, mold and exalt him—and to preserve the posterity of the Israelites.

No matter how great the trespass, you can still be set free of the wound it has caused because of the provision Jesus made at Calvary. Joseph was overcome emotionally and wept on several occasions when God finally reunited him with his family. He also wept when his brothers asked for forgiveness. I believe he wept most when the thorn or mark of what his brothers had done was heavily upon him. His weeping was God's way of releasing him from the effects of their trespasses against him, setting him free to forgive and to be free indeed!

TRUE CONFESSIONS

According to Leviticus 5, when an Israelite trespassed against someone, he had to bring a sin offering *and* a fifth of what the offering would cost as an atonement for his sin. If his offering was a lamb, for example, then he had to also bring twenty percent of what the lamb would cost and give it to the priest as his trespass offering. I believe the trespass offering was set up this way because when you are held accountable for your actions and it costs you something, you are more likely to remember the consequences of your behavior if you are ever tempted to do it again.

Jesus is our High Priest, and we can take our trespass offerings directly to Him. Once a trespass becomes a pattern of sin, however, it becomes an iniquity that is passed from generation to generation. If you'll recall from previous chapters, iniquities can only be broken by confessing them, repenting for your forefathers' participation and the part you have played in perpetuating them, and applying the blood of Jesus.

A group of people in the United States are visiting places where the American Indians were used and abused, and they are repenting and asking the Indians' forgiveness for the trespasses that both they and their forefathers committed against them. I also know of people who are going into parts of Africa and praying over places where Africans were sold into slavery. Why? Because when you repent of your trespasses, you bring a cleansing into the situation:

> **If they shall confess their iniquity, and the iniquity of their fathers, with their trespass which they trespassed against me, and that also they have walked contrary unto me; and that I also have walked contrary unto them, and have brought them into the land of their enemies; if then their**

**uncircumcised hearts be humbled, and they then
accept of the punishment of their iniquity: then will I
remember my covenant with Jacob...and I will
remember the land.**

Leviticus 26:40-42

STANDING IN THE GAP

During the period in which David was fleeing from Saul, it
was his custom to protect the sheep of a man named Nabal from
the thieves and robbers who would attempt to steal them. It was
sheep-shearing time, and Nabal was hosting a huge celebration.
David and his men were hungry.

David sent ten of his men to Nabal and asked, "Could you
possibly share some of your sheep with us? My men and I have
a need, and after all, we've helped protect both your men and
your sheep." Nabal, being the arrogant and haughty person that
he was, responded by saying:

**Who is David? ...Shall I then take my bread, and
my water, and my flesh that I have killed for my
shearers, and give it unto men, whom I know not
whence they be?**

1 Samuel 25:10,11

When David's men told him of Nabal's response, David
prepared for war. However, when Abigail, Nabal's wife, heard
what had happened, she immediately went to meet David and
his band to intercede on behalf of her husband:

Then Abigail made haste, and took two hundred loaves, and two bottles of wine, and five sheep ready dressed, and five measures of parched corn, and an hundred clusters of raisins, and two hundred cakes of figs, and laid them on asses.

1 Samuel 25:18

When she saw David and his four hundred men, she jumped off her donkey and begged him to forgive Nabal of his trespass against him. She said:

Upon me, my lord, upon me let this iniquity be.... Forgive the trespass of thine handmaid: for the Lord will certainly make my lord a sure house; because my lord fighteth the battles of the Lord, and evil hath not been found in thee all thy days.

1 Samuel 25:24,28

Abigail said, "Let my husband's trespass come on me." I'm sure many people would say, "I have enough problems of my own to contend with, so I don't need to take responsibility for my spouse's as well. He's big enough to take up for himself. I'll just be a rich widow. I'll buy a yacht and sail around the world." Instead, Abigail stood in the gap for her husband, confessed his sin and trespass as though they were her own, and brought a cleansing into the situation by bridging the gap between David and Nabal.

Ezekiel 22:30 says, "And I sought for a man among them, that should make up the hedge, and stand in the gap before me for the land, that I should not destroy it: but I found none." If you want to see yourself or someone else released from a trespass, then stand in the gap. Because Abigail stood in the gap for Nabal, it softened David's heart, and he didn't kill Nabal. If you'll remember, God brought judgment on Nabal, and he died. Then David married Abigail, and she became a queen.

The human nature is to be a gap finder instead of a gap stander. People are so willing to point out the gaps of others instead of praying to God to forgive them for their behavior. This is what Stephen did in Acts 7:60 when he was being stoned. He could have called fire down from heaven, but he chose to look heavenward and said, "Lord, lay not this sin to their charge. And when he had said this, he fell asleep."

JESUS' PROVISION

Make a quality decision right now to forgive everyone who has ever trespassed against you according to Matthew 18:35 and Luke 17:4. Ask God to forgive them as well. Isaiah 53 says Jesus was wounded for your trespasses. You may be reading this book and you're as wounded as you can be. You keep going over and over your wounds, licking them like a child does when he's pulled the scab off a wound and it begins to bleed. You lick your wounds, and you tell everybody about them.

> Make a quality decision right now to forgive everyone who has ever trespassed against you according to Matthew 18:35 and Luke 17:4.

I know a woman who is owed some money by someone who has

failed to repay her. Every day she goes over this trespass. "This person owes me money, this person owes me money," she says. Every week she calls or writes this person to say, "You owe me X-amount of money." She licks and licks this wound and keeps it moist. But until she forgives this person of the debt owed to her, her wound will never heal.

Matthew 18:15 tells you that people are going to trespass against you and what to do when this happens. Instead of doing what most people do when someone trespasses against them, you are instructed to "go and tell him his fault between thee and him alone." I can tell you that 99 percent of Christians do not go alone and tell a brother his fault. They tell everyone else first. But God says that if somebody trespasses against you, you should confront him, not in anger, but in a spirit of reconciliation: "I don't really believe you meant to do this. But this is how it made me feel."

I don't know about you, but I don't like to confront people—and I don't like for them to confront me. I do want to be a doer of the Word, however, so I practice doing what it says. This is the only way to bring healing into a potentially lethal situation. If you don't approach your brother and attempt to clear things up, it could permanently wound or mar him.

SOWING AND REAPING

If you had a thorn in your foot and couldn't find it, you would have to depend on someone with a magnifying glass and a pair of tweezers to locate and retrieve it. Galatians 4:7 says you reap what you sow.

If you sow forgiveness, you will reap it. And as you forgive, the Word will set you free and give life to those areas that have been dead because of trespasses and overcome with weeds and thorns. The magnifying glass of the Holy Spirit will locate each thorn in your heart and pull it out. He'll purge you with the blood of Jesus and apply the balm of Gilead to those areas and make you whole.

The blood of Jesus has cleansed you and your family tree. You have broken the pattern of generational sins, and your soul has been sanctified by the washing of the water by the Word. You are healed of the trespasses committed against you and the ones you have committed against others. There is no earthly reason for you to remain bound.

You have broken those sinful patterns of your past by the name of Jesus and the blood of the Lamb, turning family iniquities into generational blessings that will continue to the thousandth generation! Blessings, not curses, are your birthright. Truly, whom the Son has set free is free indeed, and this promise is for you and the next generation!

SECTION 4

The Next Generation

15

RESPONDING TO GOD

S ometimes in some areas of our lives, we think, *Why is my faith not working? What is wrong?* We raise children to serve the Lord, and then—bang!—they go haywire at a certain age. Then we ask, "What is this? God, I've got to have some answers!"

> **He that is spiritual judgeth** [understands] **all things.**
>
> **1 Corinthians 2:15**

> **They that seek the Lord understand all things.**
>
> **Proverbs 28:5**

Many times we have to wait on the Lord, and He gives us the answer eventually. As you wait on God, as you are in the Spirit, then He opens your understanding to see what the problem is and how to get rid of it. God never just identifies a problem and then leaves you to deal with it alone. He always gives you the solution to the problem and often the miracle that can turn it around.

SETTING OUR GENERATIONS FREE

Deuteronomy 28:46 is an unusual verse:

And they shall be upon thee for a sign and for a wonder, and upon thy seed for ever.

Unlike the signs and wonders in the New Testament, this Scripture refers to bad types of signs and wonders. It says that these curses which come from generation to generation will be signs and wonders of the demonic power of sin and the power of the devil to keep curses perpetuating on throughout a family's history.

Now we know the way to change things for the better! We have been bound for years by the devil, but now not only can we be set free, but also we can set our generations free! We can overcome those nasty familiar spirits and set ourselves free and our children free and our children's children free to a thousand generations, Deuteronomy 7:9 tells us.

We know that we can spoil the devil's stronghold in our households by binding him in the name of Jesus, by telling him that he can't do those awful things to our house or to our generation or to the generations that follow us.

Those evil spirits that are familiar with your family for generations know that you are already born with a weakness. When it's time, they make their attack on you. But you bind the devil, and you're not going to be a diabetic! You bind him, and you're not going to get into sexual sin! You bind him, and you're not going to live in poverty!

But remember: once you are cleansed, he's going to come back and try to take your children. If he gets them, he's going to make them seven times worse! But we don't have to let it happen to our children: We can set them free too! We don't have to put up with it any more.

RELEASING BITTERNESS

Did you know that God wants you to be free? Did you know that the Word always brings freedom?

Where the Spirit of the Lord is, there is liberty.

2 Corinthians 3:17

God wants to set you free in every area of your life. He wants you to go kick the devil in the teeth: KUNG-FU -IT

Looking diligently lest any man fail of the grace of God; lest any root of bitterness springing up trouble you, and thereby many be defiled.

Hebrews 12:15

white crane spreads ITS wings

With all that we've learned, it's pretty easy for us to read this verse and say, "Yes, that's right. Bitterness is definitely a cause of family curses. People who are bitter because of something bad that happened to their father or their great-grandfather are probably not going to get very far with family blessings. They've got to get rid of that bitterness."

Well, that's very true. But the cure for bitterness is forgiveness, and that's one attribute most people have a problem with: true, deep, from-the-heart, long-lasting forgiveness—the kind that also forgets:

> **I, even I, am he that blotteth out thy transgressions for mine own sake, and will not remember thy sins.**
>
> **Isaiah 43:25**

> **Whereby are given unto us exceeding great and precious promises: that by these ye might be partakers of the divine nature, having escaped the corruption that is in the world through lust.**
>
> **2 Peter 1:4**

Forgiveness is a divine attribute. But we now have the nature of God in us, and that makes us partakers of all His divine attributes, including genuine forgiveness.

ESAU AGAIN

> **And the boys grew: and Esau was a cunning hunter, a man of the field; and Jacob was a plain man, dwelling in tents.**
>
> **Genesis 25:27**

Looking diligently lest any man fail of the grace of God; lest any root of bitterness springing up trouble you, and thereby many be defiled; lest there be any fornicator, or profane person, as Esau, who for one morsel of meat sold his birthright. For ye know how that afterward, when he would have inherited the blessing, he was rejected: for he found no place of repentance, though he sought it carefully with tears.

Hebrews 12:15-17

There is more that we can learn from the life of Esau. He was a profane man. When I read that phrase, I thought, *What's profane? Does that mean he used profanity, that he cursed a lot?*

The Bible says that "Esau was a cunning hunter, a man of the field." From that, I think of Esau as being a "macho man"— one of those guys who likes to hunt, fish, and wrestle with the boys. "Jacob was a plain man, dwelling in tents." Jacob sounds like a mild-mannered type, more likely to engage in intellectual conversation with the ladies of the camp. The two brothers— who were twins—couldn't have been more different!

But here *profane* doesn't necessarily refer to Esau's language. It means that he was worldly, that he was very earth-conscious. He was an earthy person. When he woke up in the morning, he thought, *What's for breakfast? What am I going to eat all day?*

His whole concern was for his physical body. He was proud of his hairy chest and his strong arms that could pull a bow. He was proud of his ability to run fast and wrestle everything down. His physical prowess made his father proud of him too. But Rebekah favored the gentle Jacob.

However, Esau's preoccupation with his physique and with his ego led him to be a fornicator. Fornication can either involve sexual sin, or there can be spiritual fornication. Esau went after idols—his own ego included—rather than after the living God. He treated spiritual things very lightly.

One day he came in from a hard day of hunting, horseback riding, and other "macho man" activities, and he was hungry. There was his brother Jacob stirring a pot of stew.

Now remember that Esau was always thinking of his stomach, always thinking of his physical comforts. He said to Jacob, "I would like what you're cooking."

Jacob answered, "Well, I would like your birthright, so let's just swap." Frankly, that wasn't very nice of Jacob to suggest such a thing, to respond to Esau's insignificant moment of hunger by countering with one of the powerful things of God.

That goes to show that the devil is always on the prowl, "seeking whom he may devour" (1 Peter 5:8), just waiting for us to mistreat the holy things of God in a moment of jesting or lightheartedness, because then he can pervert God's plan for our lives. We have to be on guard, to bring "into captivity every thought to the obedience of Christ" (2 Cor. 10:5); and "whatsoever ye do in word or deed, do all in the name of the Lord Jesus" (Col. 3:17). When Jacob answered Esau with "I want your birthright," he was about to change the course of history forever!

Esau sold his birthright for a piece of meat. After he did that—after he ate all the stew and was lying around with a comfortably full belly—then he felt bad about it. But he didn't repent to God. He didn't say, "Dear God, You've given me so much! How could I have treated the gift that You gave me so lightly?" He just felt sorry that he had missed out on a bargain.

We can be sorry that we get caught in sin but not sorry that we sinned and hurt God or even hurt other people. We're just sorry for the consequences. That is not godly repentance. It does not bring forth the faithful or beautiful fruits of righteousness.

THE CURSE OF DEPRESSION

Do you know what most depression is? Earthly sorrow. You are in sin when you're depressed.

(Of course, not *all* depression is sin. In some cases, it may be a spiritual attack. That you have authority to stand against every attack of the devil. In other cases, depression can be the result of a chemical imbalance. But thank God, He can heal you and deliver you from it. Again, if you need to, talk to your pastor or someone at your church—or your doctor may even be able to help.)

People want to be petted when they're depressed. "Oh, be nice to me, treat me sweetly because I'm depressed." They are really on one of those "Woe is me! Pity me!" kicks. But the

Lord is not going to sympathize with you because depression is unbelief, and unbelief is a sin!

Often depression is unconfessed sin. You didn't deal with it yourself, thinking somebody else has treated you wrongly. But the root of depression can be giving in to sin, and that's a curse. It can lead to mental and emotional breakdown. It can lead to serious psychotic disorders. It can even lead to insanity. And it can be passed from one generation to the next.

Esau lost his birthright, and he also lost his blessing. Jacob just sailed in and grabbed the blessing. Jacob was wrong in the way he did it, and so was Rebekah. But their opportunity was created because of Esau's sin.

Esau lost his birthright, he lost his blessing, and then he ran into Isaac's tent and cried. He said, "Oh, Daddy, I've lost my birthright!" Whose fault was it? It was Esau's own fault, but he didn't say that. "Oh, Daddy, I've lost my blessing! Please, please! I feel so sorry about this!" This is earthly sorrow. "Please, don't you have another blessing?"

He was trying to get his father to relent and give him a blessing. But he never got it. He got just a little of the leftover blessing. "He sought it with tears," but he never got it.

Esau did not use godly sorrow; he used earthly sorrow. If he had used godly sorrow, he would have said, "God, how I failed, and how I blew it!" Instead he said, "God, how Jacob failed, and how he blew it! And look at my mother; she's not even for me! They failed me!"

Esau became bitter in his heart against his brother and against his mother—although the Word says, "Honour thy father and thy mother" (Deut. 5:16)—and probably a little against God too. Esau never used the godly repentance which would have cleansed him and set him free. He became defiled by his bitterness when he could have reversed the curse by repenting of his part in it.

That's the difference. We want everybody else to repent, but we think we don't need to because we're so sweet. "Why should I have to repent? I didn't do anything that bad."

Esau sold the birthright, so he obviously didn't think that the blessing was too important. Later he wanted to murder Jacob for what he had done. "It's Jacob's fault! It's Mama's fault!" He was so wrapped up in his self-pity that he never realized that godly repentance would remove his fault and change the situation!

As long as you cop out, you will experience depression, and you will experience bitterness. When you are bitter, you defile yourself, and you may defile others as well. Esau defiled his generations, which is a tragedy.

BITTER FATHERS—BITTER CHILDREN

Bitterness is a luxury you cannot afford. It's too expensive. It will defile you, and it will defile those around you:

The fathers have eaten a sour grape, and the children's teeth are set on edge.

Jeremiah 31:29

That's exactly what happened to Esau. When Esau became bitter against Jacob and Jacob's descendants, his children became bitter against Jacob's descendants too:

And Moses sent messengers from Kadesh unto the king of Edom, Thus saith thy brother Israel, Thou knowest all the travail that hath befallen us: How our fathers went down into Egypt, and we have dwelt in Egypt a long time; and the Egyptians vexed us, and our fathers: and when we cried unto the Lord, he heard our voice, and sent an angel, and hath brought us forth out of Egypt: and, behold, we are in Kadesh, a city in the uttermost of thy border: let us pass, I pray thee, through thy country: we will not pass through the fields, or through the vineyards, neither will we drink of the water of the wells: we will go by the king's high way, we will not turn to the right hand nor to the left, until we have passed thy borders.

And Edom said unto him, Thou shalt not pass by me, lest I come out against thee with the sword. And the children of Israel said unto him, We will go by the high way: and if I and my raffle drink of thy water; then I will pay for it: I will only, without doing any thing else, go through on my feet. And he said, Thou shalt not go through. And Edom came out against him with much people, and with a strong hand. Thus Edom refused to give Israel passage

**through his border: wherefore Israel turned away
from him.**

Numbers 20:14-21

Edom was the country that belonged to Esau and his
descendants. When the Israelites came out of Egypt, they said,
"We need to pass through Edom on our way to the Promised
Land. If you will let us pass through, we will pay for the water
that our animals drink and that we drink. We will pay for the
grass that they eat. We will pay for everything."

But the Edomites said, "No! We hate the descendants of
Jacob. You can't come through here." What did the descendants
of Jacob themselves ever do to the Edomites? Nothing! This was
over four hundred years after Jacob got Esau's blessing! But the
Edomites were bitter. Their "teeth were set on edge" because of
Esau's bitterness against Jacob.

You may be bitter against someone. It may go back into
your childhood, when some teacher yelled at you in school—or
when the factory closed down and your father lost his job, and
you had to get an after-school job to contribute to the family's
income. Maybe your husband is all wrapped up in his job, and
you're becoming bitter because it looks like he cares more about
his work than he does about you.

If you are bitter against someone, you can't afford it! It's
going to cost you your blessing. And it can cost your children's
blessing too. You had better repent. You are wrong to be bitter,
and you're going to live in depression and defeat until you do.

> *If you are bitter against someone, you can't afford it! It's going to cost you your blessing. And it can cost your children's blessing too.*

This bitterness followed Esau all the way down through his descendants. Saul had a problem with Esau's descendants. David had a problem with the Edomites. Practically every king of Judah and some of the kings of the Northern Kingdom had trouble with Esau's seed. They were always interfering with Jacob's descendants and giving them a hard time. Why? Because their father "ate sour grapes," and all the generations' teeth were set on edge.

In the New Testament, the Idumeans were descendants of the Edomites as well. The four Herods were Idumean, which means they were Edomites too.

Did they say, "Oh, here comes Jesus! We just love Jesus. We want to serve Jesus!" They never said that. Herod the Great said, "Where is He? I want to worship Him," (Matt. 2:8)—but he didn't want to worship Jesus; he wanted to kill Him!

So Herod had all the male Jewish babies under two years of age murdered. Why? Because he had bitterness toward any of God's seed. It began with Esau, and hundreds of years later Herod's teeth were still set on edge.

Herod could have repented. He had heard the Word from the wise men, and he knew of the miraculous star. The instant he would have repented, that generational curse could have been broken!

The instant you repent of your sins, the curse is broken. But as long as you cop out, as long as you dump the blame on everybody else and what you think they've done to you, then the curse will *not* be broken in your life.

> *The instant you repent of your sins, the curse is broken.*

You will continue to be depressed. You will continue to be bitter. And you will sow sourness in the lives of others. It's not worth it.

As we've seen, each of the four Herods in the Bible had his chance to repent and break that long-standing curse. Each one of them heard God's Word—and a couple of them were "almost persuaded"—but they ended up turning their backs on God instead. They committed some horrible crimes—including murdering several thousand babies—thus fulfilling their part in the family curse.

After four generations of trying to save the Herodian family from their cursed Canaanite heritage, God said, "Enough." And the last Herod died. There are no more Herods around today either!

If you are almost persuaded to repent of your sins, your "almost" is not enough, and you will be a failure. You stand to lose everything—your entire family may die out!—if you don't stop those generational curses right now.

You must say, "I repent of everything. I'm not going to hold bitterness in my heart." And then when you repent, you are free, and the generational curse is broken. You can free the next generation so that something seven times worse won't come upon them. Don't be like Esau who ate sour grapes and defiled all of his generations.

THE RIGHT WAY

Now let me tell you something not to do at this point: don't go up to somebody at church and say, "I've been bitter against you for months; please forgive me," if that person didn't even know you had felt that way!

He will think, *My, my! What did I do?* Then you walk away all forgiven, and the person becomes heartsick. If someone doesn't know he's offended you, then be quiet about it and go to God with it instead of creating another problem.

But if the person does know about your offense, especially if you've been ugly with him, then it doesn't matter what he's done—you get free before God, and you get free before him! Job got free with both God and man, and then his captivity was turned.

THE BEST ATTITUDE

To the hungry soul every bitter thing is sweet.

Proverbs 27:7

If you are hungry for God, then you will not become bitter. You will make the bitter things sweet. If you're hungry for God and somebody is mean to you, you'll say, "Well, God, here's Your opportunity to make my friend at peace with me, because "when a man's ways please the Lord, he maketh even his enemies to be at peace with him" (Prov. 16:7).

"You're calling him a *friend?*" someone else might say.

Yes, that "enemy" is a friend "to the hungry soul," to the man or woman who is hungry after God. Do you know what happens to the hungry soul when trouble comes? He thinks that God is getting ready to give him a bigger miracle!

Are you in a financial crisis? Then praise God—and don't become bitter—because you're about to get a miracle! You make the choice. You decide what is going to happen to you, whether you're going to allow this attack on your finances to continue. Maybe it's a generational curse trying to latch onto you, but you have the choice to stop the devil in his tracks.

TURN CURSES INTO BLESSINGS

The biggest miracles in my life didn't come when everything was going smoothly. People weren't saying, "That Marilyn Hickey, isn't she just great!" No, they were saying, "What is she doing? She must be crazy!" Why? Because during the greatest financial crisis our ministry has ever faced, God opened the door for us to go on daily television.

When the financial pressure was on, the devil was hitting us with strife and everything under the sun, and I thought, *God, where is the nearest bridge? I'll shoot myself and just fall over backward so I can't miss.*

But God kept telling me, "Hang in with Me. Stay in the Spirit, and you will get a miracle!"

It was during that time that God gave us the biggest miracle we've ever had in our ministry. Why? Because "to the hungry soul every bitter thing is sweet," and God knows how to reverse the curse!

The answer wasn't for me to quit. The answer was for me to say, "God, I'm so hungry for You. What miracle do *You* have for this situation?" Then I watched Him come on the scene and do something out of this world!

16

THE HERITAGE OF
THE RECHABITES

Now let's look at an example of a man who responded to God—and whose descendants were blessed for thousands of generations!

> **And when he [Jehu] was departed thence, he lighted on Jehonadab the son of Rechab coming to meet him: and he saluted him, and said to him, Is thine heart right, as my heart is with thy heart? And Jehonadab answered, It is....**
>
> **2 Kings 10:15**

Jehonadab, the son of Rechab, lived in Israel in the days of Ahab and Jezebel. In spite of all the idolatry going on around him, Jehonadab loved God very much, and he hated what was going on. So he rebelled against Ahab and Jezebel.

As Ahab and Jezebel reigned over the Northern Kingdom, continuing to lead the people in idolatry, Jehonadab said, "I'm not going to have my children under the influence of idolatry and Baal worship," so he left the city of Samaria.

JEHONADAB — THE MAN WHO RESPONDED TO GOD

Then God spoke to him, "If you will be true to Me, there are three things I'm going to require of you: that you not drink anything of the vine, that you not buy any land, and that you become a nomad and make your living from shepherding goats and sheep. Teach your children this way, and I will protect your household, and they will never be involved in idolatry."

About this time civil war broke out in Israel. Ahaziah became the king, but he had to fight to keep his throne. Then a man named Jehu came upon the scene. He had been anointed by Elisha to go into Israel and cut off the house of Ahab and take the throne of the Northern Kingdom.

Jehu was the son of Jehoshaphat, the son of Nimshi; and one from the prophets' school anointed him king. So Jehu was anointed by God's prophet, and he had all the right people on his side.

Then Jehu came to Jehonadab and said, "Would you go with me and help me kill the priests of Baal and Jezebel?" And Jehonadab agreed. They concocted a scheme to lure all of the worshipers of Baal together in one place. Then they slew them. (2 Kings 10:18-25.)

But before that, Jehu took care of the root of idolatry in the Northern Kingdom:

> **And when Jehu was come to Jezreel, Jezebel heard of it; and she painted her face, and tired her head, and looked out at a window. And as Jehu entered in at the gate, she said, Had Zimri peace, who slew his master? And he lifted up his face to the window, and said, Who is on my side? who? And there looked out to him two or three eunuchs. And he said, Throw her down. So they threw her down: and some of her blood was sprinkled on the wall, and on the horses: and he trode her under foot.**
>
> **2 Kings 9:30-33**

As old as she was then, Jezebel still painted her eyes and arranged her hair; then she went to look out the palace window. She looked down at Jehu and asked, "What do you want?"

Jehu answered, "I want you to die."

Jezebel laughed, "Oh, you know what happened to the last man who rebelled against the king."

But there were some eunuchs standing up there with her, and Jehu commanded, "Push her over." And they did. She fell, and the dogs of the city ate her body, except for the skull, the feet, and the palms of her hands, just as had been prophesied.

Then Jehu went in and had dinner—can you imagine eating after that spectacle? They decided to bury what was left of Jezebel, giving her honors because she was a king's daughter. However, there was little left to bury. (2 Kings 8:34-37.)

In the meantime, here is Jehonadab, who had proven that he was true to God. God said to him, "If you will keep your generations correct—if you will teach each generation—then I will protect them from these curses. They shall not get into idolatry."

The way we live is serious. What we do affects our children and our grandchildren. Once the curses are broken, we must continue following God in order to keep the curses broken. When we walk in righteousness, the next generation and the next are going to be blessed because of us. The earth will be blessed because "righteousness exalteth a nation" (Prov. 14:34).

THE PEOPLE WHO REMAINED FAITHFUL TO GOD

Go unto the house of the Rechabites, and speak unto them, and bring them into the house of the Lord, into one of the chambers and give them wine to dring.... And I [Jeremiah] said unto them, Drink ye wine. But they said, we will drink no wine: for Jonadab the son of Rechab our father commanded us, saying, ye shall drink no wine...neither shall ye build house, nor sow seed, nor plant vineyard...but all your days ye shall dwell in tents....

And Jeremiah said unto the house of the Rechabites, Thus saith the Lord of hosts, the God of

Israel; Because ye have obeyed the commandment of Jonadab [Jehonadab] **your father, and kept all his precepts, and done according unto all that he hath commanded you: therefore thus saith the Lord of hosts, the God of Israel; Jonadab the son of Rechab shall not want a man to stand before me for ever.**
Jeremiah 35:2,5-7,18,19

Years later Jeremiah (who was called the "weeping prophet"), was down in the Southern Kingdom, crying and weeping over Judah because they'd gone astray.

One day God told Jeremiah, "Call in the princes of Judah, and call in the Rechabites." The latter were Jehonadab's people because he was the son of Rechab. The Rechabites were Jehonadab's children and grandchildren, several generations later. God told Jeremiah, "Call in the Rechabites and pour wine for all of them. Have the princes of Judah come in and watch."

So Jeremiah called in all the Rechabites and seated them at a table of honor. He poured wine for each of them.

But didn't God tell Jehonadab that his seed were not to drink wine? That's right. There were three things God had commanded Jehonadab and his seed: they were not to drink wine, they were not to buy land, and they were to be nomads.

So what was Jeremiah doing when he poured wine for them? These were godly people, and he was a prophet! Why was he tempting them?

God was teaching a lesson to two groups of people that day: to the Rechabites and to the princes of Judah who had gone astray. Jeremiah poured the wine for the Rechabites right in front of the Judaean princes and said, "Go ahead, you sons of Jehonadab, have a drink."

But they answered, "No, we can't drink. We have a vow to God. We're going to serve God from generation to generation. We're not going to drink wine, not even a little friendly glass on special occasions. And we're not going to own land, and we're going to continue to be a nomadic people."

Jeremiah smiled one of his rare smiles and said, "But go ahead, have a drink! I've poured it for you already."

The Rechabites answered, "No, we can't."

Then Jeremiah turned to the princes of Judah and said, "Do you see these people? They made a family promise to serve God. They're going to serve Him no matter what happens. They are just the seed of Jehonadab, but they're remaining faithful to God.

"However, you are the seed of David, and you're breaking all of the laws that God has given, the laws that are to be a blessing to your generation! You're turning your blessings into curses!"

Jeremiah continued, "How could you turn your blessings into curses? These people have been true to God in their simple way. Why can't you be true to the way of God Himself, so that the Messiah can come through your seed?" (Jer. 36:1-8.)

Jeremiah used the Rechabites as an example to the princes of Judah, but they still did not yield.

The Rechabites had the right idea. They refused to yield to pressure, even when it seemed to be coming from a righteous source. Yes, they were tested, but they refused to submit to alcohol. They wouldn't even be "social drinkers."

Do you know that alcohol destroys your brain cells? You need all of your brain cells! No one is so smart that he can stand to lose a few. Wally and I have seen people who once were brilliant become mental vegetables because they became alcoholics.

Parents who are social drinkers set a double standard for their children. They say to their children, "Now, don't drink." But then the children see their folks laughing it up with a glass of wine or a can of beer in their hands. Parents, don't try to teach your children not to drink when you do it yourself. You don't want your child to be an alcoholic, so throw those wine bottles out!

THE PROMISES OF GOD ARE EVERLASTING

After Jeremiah admonished the princes of Judah, he turned and prophesied to the children of Jehonadab. He said, "Because you have been true to God, when Nebuchadnezzar comes in here and destroys Judah, he will not take you captive. Your children will be free, and your grandchildren will be free. They will never go into captivity."

Then he prophesied to the princes of Judah, "But you princes of Judah! Your children will be eunuchs. They will be taken into captivity and murdered. They will be killed, and you will have no further generations because you would not judge yourselves and judge your own sin."

God's final word to the sons of Jehonadab was this: "You shall never lack a descendant to stand before Me!" Isn't that a beautiful promise?

Now let me tell you what happened to the Rechabites. They lived in the Northern Kingdom when Assyria came down and attacked Israel. The Assyrians took all the people captive except the Rechabites, because they weren't there! They were nomads, and they had gone down to Judah at that time because of a famine. They were safe with all their sheep, their lambs, and their oxen. They missed the Assyrian captivity! Now that's divine protection.

Then years later, when Nebuchadnezzar conquered Judah, he told his soldiers, "Leave the nomads alone." So the Rechabites were never taken into captivity by the Assyrians or by the Babylonians.

The seed of Jehonadab didn't fall apart because they were true to God. You can't curse what God has blessed! If you are walking in the Word of God, then you are walking in the blessings of God, and a curse will not be able to come upon you or your generations. You're not here to be cursed because you are here to reverse the curse!

Now, I've saved the best part for last. Do you know that there are Rechabites living in Jericho today? The Rechabite lineage has not ended, and they are still serving the God of their fathers. That's generation after generation after generation after generation of blessed people! God said, "Those that love Me, I will bless them to the thousandth generation!" The Rechabites are living proof that serving God and walking in His Word brings a blessing into your life and continues that blessing on down through your generations, breaking the curse of the past!

17

THE HOUSE OF RIGHTEOUSNESS

So you want to be free from generational curses, and you want to clean up your act right now. You're willing to forgive those who have gone before you and passed down their curses to you. You're willing to forgive those people who have hurt you today, and you're going to pray for them rather than be bitter against them. You want your children and your children's children to inherit only blessings from you.

WATCH OUT FOR THESE!

He that troubleth his own house shall inherit the wind.

Proverbs 11:29

I used to think that the phrase "inheriting the wind" meant that you would get an empty handful of nothing. You cannot hold onto wind! But I've since learned that if you are violent to your wife or cruel to your children or hateful with your words, if you gripe about the things of God, then you are going to inherit the wind—but it will be a hurricane:

> **Therefore whosoever heareth these sayings of mine, and doeth them, I will liken him unto a wise man, which built his house upon a rock: and the rain descended, and the floods came and the winds blew, and beat upon that house; and it fell not: for it was founded upon a rock.**
>
> **And every one that heareth these sayings of mine, and doeth them not, shall be likened unto a foolish man, which built his house upon the sand: and the rain descended, and the floods came, and the winds blew, and beat upon that house; and it fell: and great was the fall of it.**
>
> **Matthew 7:24-27**

If your house is built on sand and not on the solid rock of the Word, then it's going to blow down. Don't gripe at God. Don't gripe at the church. Don't gripe at other Christians, because in so doing you are troubling your own house:

> **He that is greedy of gain troubleth his own house.**
>
> **Proverbs 15:27**

What does that mean? "Greedy of gain" is actually idolatry. It's saying, "I'd rather make money than go to church. I'd rather make money than go to early morning prayer." This refers to what your true priorities are. But the following is godly priority.

But seek ye first the kingdom of God, and his righteousness; and all these things shall be added unto you.

Matthew 6:33

If the pursuit of riches and wealth is more important to you than promoting the kingdom of God, then you are into idolatry, and idolatry is a terrible sin.

Do you remember what God said would happen to idolaters?

Thou shalt have none other gods before me.... Thou shalt not bow down thyself unto them, nor serve them: for I the Lord thy God am a jealous God, visiting the iniquity of the fathers upon the children unto the third and fourth generation of them that hate me.

Deuteronomy 5:7,9

What kind of curse does idolatry bring?

But it shall come to pass, if thou wilt not hearken unto the voice of the Lord thy God...the Lord shall send upon thee cursing, vexation, and rebuke, in all that thou settest thine hand unto for to do, until thou be destroyed, and until thou perish quickly; because

of the wickedness of thy doings, whereby thou hast
forsaken me.

Deuteronomy 28:15,20

If that isn't scary enough, read this:

The Lord shall make the pestilence cleave unto
thee, until he have consumed thee from off the
land.... The Lord shall smite thee with a
consumption, and with a fever, and with an
inflammation, and with an extreme burning, and
with the sword, and with blasting, and with mildew;
and they shall pursue thee until thou perish.

Deuteronomy 28:21,22

These are the sort of curses that come upon you if you turn
to idolatry—and they will come upon your children and upon
your children's children too!

Another form of idolatry is the pursuit of fame and power,
the attitude, "I want an important position." The lust for power
is idolatry. True recognition actually comes from the Lord:

But God is the judge: he putteth down one, and
setteth up another.

Psalm 75:7

So then it is not of him that willeth, nor of him
that runneth, but of God that sheweth mercy.

Romans 9:16

If you spend your time trying to gain public acceptance and popularity, then you're going to see a backlash in your own family. Chasing fame is idolatry, and the curse of that sin is going to overtake you.

It's going to overtake your children and your future generations because they will inherit your weakness. They will be prey to the familiar spirits that are just watching and waiting for their turn to strike at the next generation. And most likely your children will be seven times worse than you are.

> *If you spend your time trying to gain public acceptance and popularity, then you're going to see a backlash in your own family.*

Whoso rewardeth evil for good, evil shall not depart from his house.

Proverbs 17:13

That means that if you work for a good employer but sow evil back to your employer, watch out! Remember what Paul wrote about that:

And whatsoever ye do, do it heartily, as to the Lord, and not unto men.

Colossians 3:23

"Well, I just don't like that person," you say. It doesn't matter if you like that person or not—if you reward evil for good, then you're bringing a curse upon yourself. If those people have been good to you, but then you turn around and speak against them—watch out!

When Wally and I were assistant pastors of a church in Amarillo, Texas, we experienced a situation with the church secretary. She gossiped too much, and she was bitter about many things; she generally had a bad attitude.

Wally and I were young, and this was our first time in the ministry. This woman began telling us negative things, and we started allowing it into our spirits, our minds, and our emotions. Then we started speaking negatively ourselves.

When God called us out to have our own church, pretty soon we noticed some people were doing to us what we had done to the other pastor. Do you know what I did? I repented! I said, "I will never disrespect the hand that feeds me. I will never do that again!"

That pastor hadn't hurt us at all; he was good to us. But I learned never to reward evil for good by picking up somebody else's offenses. That's a sin, and it brings a curse on me and on my household. You know that I repented! When I saw that man later, I could look him full in his face and think, *I'm clean! Glory to God, I'm clean!*

STRIVE FOR THESE!

The house of the righteous shall stand.

Proverbs 12:7

That's what we're trying to achieve! We are "the righteousness of God in him [Christ]" (2 Cor. 5:21). We are freed from generational curses, and we shall stand:

Through wisdom is an house builded.

Proverbs 24:3

A WORD TO WOMEN

Every wise woman buildeth her house: but the foolish plucketh it down with her hands.

Proverbs 14:1

Ladies, what do you say to your children about their father? Do you say, "I wish he made more money. I wish he weren't so fat. I wish he'd fix all these things that are broken around here. I wish he'd do something about his car—I'm tired of this old wreck. I wish he'd go to church, that big thug!"

If that's the way you talk about your husband to your children, then you're not a wise woman. You've got bitterness in your heart, and you're pouring it into your children.

Maybe you've been divorced and you're deeply wounded by your former spouse. Do you want to pour that bitterness out into your children? Do you know what will happen? Your little girl will pour out the same bitterness on her husband, and perhaps her marriage will end in divorce just like yours did.

This is a real battle! We're dealing with serious things. This isn't a cupcake factory or an old people's home or a country club—this is a spiritual war! If we fight the battle God's way, then wonderful victories will follow:

Let all bitterness, and wrath, and anger...be put away from you.

Ephesians 4:31

Don't pour your hurts and wounds out on your children—pour them out on Jesus, and let Him heal you. Then pour out love and wisdom on your kids. By wisdom the house is built.

A WORD TO MEN

Husbands, love your wives, and be not bitter against them.

Colossians 3:19

Why is it so bad to be bitter against your wife? What do you think about your wife? "That fat slob. I wish she could make a decent gravy, like my mother can. I wish she were a better Christian. I wish she'd keep the house cleaner. I wish she were a better lover."

Well, maybe you need to be a better lover yourself! Do you ever tell her that you love her and that she looks good?

Husband, don't be bitter against your wife, because we've already seen what bitterness does: you defile yourself. You defile your home, and you'll destroy your son's chance for a successful marriage if that's the way you talk. Instead, build a house of righteousness.

STAYING FREE

Don't put up with the devil's lies and curses. If he comes with symptoms of something that you've already broken, you need to go after him again! One mistake Christians make is thinking they only have one battle to fight. That's not true! The devil will come at you with the same thing time after time; you'll be set free from the symptoms, and he'll come back again. But God's Word says,

Greater is he that is in you, than he that is in the world.

1 John 4:4

You've got to blast the devil with the Word and with your faith. You may have to use it on your children. Tell them, "This is what the Word says, this is what the Word says!" Keep on fighting the enemy until you win. Don't give up—stay with it until you win.

You can be free from any curse that has invaded your life. You don't have to continue under the curse that your father or your grandfather or your great-grandfather sent down to your generation. Your children don't have to be under any of the curses either. You can reverse the curse, turning it into a blessing that will continue to the thousandth generation! And you can build a house of righteousness.

$$\boxed{18}$$

BEGINNING YOUR
HERITAGE OF BLESSINGS

In this chapter we will examine some very specific things you can do to begin your heritage of blessings. Yes, *you* can directly impact the spiritual growth of your family and cause it to grow in good soil with a strong, healthy root system that will produce life and not death. If you have already followed the steps to cleanse your family tree through personal and national repentance, forgiveness, and the shed blood of Jesus, then you have begun a process that will reap eternal benefits.

I like to use the analogy of a plant that is dying because it is planted in poor soil. Similarly, once a family tree is cleansed of its iniquities, it, too, must be repotted from the "bad," unfruitful soil of the past to the new, fertile soil of Jesus Christ. Once you've completed this process, you can begin to focus on establishing blessings for this and the next generation, maintaining these blessings, and nurturing a mature family tree.

THE GOOD SOIL

In nature, to grow a healthy, mature tree, the tree must be planted in good, fertile soil. The same is true for your family tree. To begin a heritage of blessings, you must plant the seed of God's Word in your own heart as well as in the hearts of your family members. The spiritual seed that you plant must be planted in "good" ground, which in God's kingdom is symbolized by the heart. It is in the heart that the Word of God is planted, and it is in the heart that the Word of God bears much, little, or no fruit. Jesus likened the heart to the types of soil that the Word is planted in:

> **A farmer went out to sow his seed. As he was scattering the seed, some fell along the path** [the wayside]**; it was trampled on, and the birds of the air ate it up. Some fell on rock** [rocky ground]**, and when it came up, the plants withered because they had no moisture. Other seed fell among thorns, which grew up with it and choked the plants. Still other seed fell on good soil and came up and yielded a crop, a hundred times more than was sown....**
>
> **Luke 8:5-8** NIV

"This is the meaning of the parable: The seed is the word of God. Those along the path are the ones who hear, and then the devil comes and takes away the word from their hearts, so that they may not believe and be saved. Those on the rock are the ones who receive the word with joy when they hear it, but they have no root. They believe for a while, but in the time of testing they fall away. The seed that fell among thorns stands for those who hear, but as they go on their way they are choked by life's worries, riches and pleasures, and they do not mature. But the seed on good soil stands for those with a noble and good heart, who hear the word, retain it, and by persevering produce a crop."

Luke 8:11-15 NIV

The "path" or "wayside" is the first type of soil Jesus mentions. It represents a person whose understanding of the Word is in his head only and not in his heart. He mentally assents that the Word of God is true but lacks spiritual depth and understanding. Consequently, the devil has little or no difficulty stealing the Word that was sown in this person's heart.

The rocky ground is symbolic of the person who joyfully receives the Word as truth but has a superficial understanding of it. When the pressures of life and temptations come to challenge his level of commitment to be a doer of the Word he has received, he becomes fainthearted and falls away. The seed that is sown in this type of ground soon withers and dies.

The thorny ground is the third type of soil. Like the Word sown in the rocky ground, the Word of truth will also be received by the person whose heart is thorny. However, the cares, riches, and pleasures of this world choke the Word in this person and cause it to become unfruitful.

Seed sown into the good ground, according to this scripture, yields a crop one hundred times more than what was sown. This person's heart is ripe for the Word—it is pure and holy before the Father. The King James Version of Luke 8:15 says that the heart of this person is honest and good; having heard the Word, he keeps or does it and bears fruit with patience.

I once heard a well-known speaker say, "A good marriage takes work, and a bad marriage takes even more work." This same principle is true when it comes to establishing a godly family tree. Even when the seed is sown in good soil, there are things that must be done to cultivate a good crop or harvest.

As is true in nature, the soil must be cultivated before the seed you sow will reap a bountiful harvest. If you sow seed on hard, barren ground, you can expect to receive little, if any, results. As a matter of fact, one of the purposes of praise and worship in our church services is to usher in God's presence and to prepare the congregation's hearts to receive the Word of God. Although the Word can be delivered without this cultivating process, you will find that the congregation is less receptive because they are still consumed with the thoughts and events of the day as opposed to focusing on the things of God.

Cultivating your family tree is a very simple process. All you have to do is make a quality decision and commitment to apply the Word of God to *every area* of your life. In doing this, you are uprooting any weeds of iniquity that might be present and tilling your heart and your family's hearts to receive the Word. As a seed does in nature, the seed of the Word undergoes a process; you must allow time for it to germinate, sprout, and grow before it produces the desired fruit. The more skillful you become at cultivating your heart and your family's hearts, the more fertile your hearts will become and the more fruit you will produce as you receive the good seed—God's Word.

FEEDING THE TREE

As newborn babes, desire the sincere milk of the word, that ye may grow thereby.

1 Peter 2:2

Whom shall he teach knowledge? and whom shall he make to understand doctrine? them that are weaned from the milk, and drawn from the breasts.

Isaiah 28:9

Feeding your family tree is a process that takes place over a period of time; it is not just a one-time thing. After you have sown the seed for a good family tree, you must care for and nurture it. To nurture means "to feed and protect; to nurture one's offspring; to support and encourage as during the period of training or development; to bring up; train."[1]

One of the basic ways you nurture your tree is to feed it (your family) the Word of God. This can be done through regular family devotions and Scripture memorization. You will also need to block out a certain time of day in which you discuss the Word with your family. Perhaps the best time for your family to do this is the first thing in the morning or around dinnertime. The choice is up to you. But there needs to be an emphasis on the Word in your home in addition to what your family learns at church.

You're probably thinking, *Marilyn, this is so simple! It's elementary.*

That's true, but I've discovered that some of the most profound revelations I've ever received have been simple. The Word is what will cause your family to overcome its inherited family iniquities: "And they overcame him by the blood of the Lamb, and by *the word* of their testimony" (Rev. 12:11). If you are going to feed your family spiritually, then you need to start with the Word of God.

WATERING THE TREE

In order for a tree to grow, it must be watered on a consistent basis. "How," you might ask, "do you water a family tree?" With the washing of the water by the Word—the sanctifying work of the Holy Spirit—who is symbolized in the Scriptures as rivers of living water:

> **Jesus stood and cried, saying, If any man thirst,**
> **let him come unto me, and drink. He that believeth**

**on me, as the scripture hath said, out of his belly
shall flow rivers of living water.**

John 7:37,38

The rivers of living water in John 7 refer to the Holy Spirit,
who resides in every born-again believer. (1 Cor. 3:16; 6:19.)
Because He dwells in you, you have access to the very throne
room of God:

**"But the Counselor, the Holy Spirit, whom the
Father will send in my name, will teach you all
things and will remind you of everything I have said**
[the Word you plant in your heart] **to you."**

John 14:26 NIV

**"But when he, the Spirit of truth, comes, he will
guide you into all truth. He will not speak on his
own; he will speak only what he hears, and he will
tell you what is yet to come. He will bring glory to
me by taking from what is mine and making it
known to you. All that belongs to the Father is mine.
That is why I said the Spirit will take from what is
mine and make it known to you."**

John 16:13-15 NIV

One of the many roles or functions of the Holy Spirit
according to John 14:26 NIV, is to "teach you all things, and
bring all things to your remembrance." As you and your family
study the Word of God, the Holy Spirit will give you an
understanding of the truths being presented to you and will

remind you of what you have deposited in your heart so you can apply the Word to your daily life.

This is the watering process. The Holy Spirit will water or give life and meaning to the Word as you and your family apply the Word to your daily lives. The fruit that you will bear from being watered by Him will give you insight and revelation into the mysteries of God and divine direction for your family. As you and your family plant the Word in your hearts, the Holy Spirit will water the good seed that you are planting, and it will overtake and choke out the weeds from the seeds planted by your forefathers generations ago.

In conjunction with the Holy Spirit, you and your family also have a role in the watering process. The part you and your family play can be found in James 1:22: "But be ye doers of the word, and not hearers only." In other words, as you and your family follow the leading of the Holy Spirit, you will enable Him to water the seeds that will sprout up into a good, healthy, mature family tree.

PRUNING

The pruning of a family tree is just as important as feeding and watering it. When a plant or tree is pruned, all of the dead leaves and limbs are cut off. Anger, laziness, sickness, and a bad attitude are just some examples of dead weights that the Holy Spirit will prune from your family tree.

The purpose of this pruning process is to remove everything that would hinder the natural growth process of that tree. John

15:4,16 promise that as you and your family abide in God and His Word abides in you, you will produce much fruit and your fruit shall remain. Additionally we read:

> **I am the True Vine and My Father is the Vinedresser. Any branch in Me that does not bear fruit—that stops bearing—He cuts away (trims off, takes away). And He cleanses and repeatedly prunes every branch that continues to bear fruit, to make it bear more and richer and more excellent fruit.**
>
> **John 15:1,2 AMP**

We know from nature that whenever you plant something, such as a flower garden, both the good and the bad seed—the weeds—come up together. I've spent many a summer afternoon weeding my garden, but thank God for the Holy Spirit who does the separating and pruning of our spiritual family trees:

> **"The kingdom of heaven is like a man who sowed good seed in his field. But while everyone was sleeping, his enemy came and sowed weeds among the wheat, and went away. When the wheat sprouted and formed heads, then the weeds also appeared. The owner's servants came to him and said, Sir, didn't you sow good seed in your field? Where then did the weeds come from? An enemy did this, he replied.... 'Let both grow together until the harvest. At that time I will tell the harvesters: First collect the**

weeds and tie them in bundles to be burned; then gather the wheat and bring it into my barn.'"

Matthew 13:24-28,30 NIV

As you plant the seed of God's Word in the hearts of you and your family and allow the Holy Spirit to water it, bad seed or family iniquities may surface from time to time. Be assured, however, that a time of separation will come, and the iniquities of the past will be consumed by the Word of God, thus enabling your family to inherit and pass on generational blessings.

I was a schoolteacher when I became Spirit-filled. I was teaching a literature class, and I read two or three books a week. I loved to read, but the Lord told me to quit reading fiction and to use that time to read the Bible instead. I was obedient and began memorizing one book of the Bible a year.

Although I was unaware of it at the time, God was pruning me during this period of my life. My husband and I didn't know we were called into the ministry. We were newlyweds, but God was getting us ready for the time when He would use us in the ministry.

I can look back now and see the pruning times in my life. God said I had some attitudes that I had to get rid of because they would hinder the call of God on my life. I knew I either had to let Him prune me, or my vines would wither and be fruitless.

NURTURING THE TREE FOR FUTURE GENERATIONS

David had a very fruitful family tree. He fed, watered, and pruned it. Although he committed adultery and murder, his repentance turned a family iniquity into a generational blessing.

Psalm 32 was written after David's sin with Bathsheba and his transgression against Uriah the Hittite were revealed. David dealt with three kinds of sin in this psalm: the sin of "missing the mark" when he had Uriah killed; the sin of transgression when he and Bathsheba committed adultery; and the sin of iniquity when he attempted to cover his sin and not confess it:

> *David had a very fruitful family tree. He fed, watered, and pruned it.*

Blessed is he whose transgression is forgiven, whose sin is covered. Blessed is the man unto whom the Lord imputeth not iniquity, and in whose spirit there is no guile. When I kept silence, my bones waxed old through my groaning all the day long. For day and night thy hand was heavy upon me: my moisture is turned into the drought of summer.... I acknowledged my sin unto thee, and mine iniquity have I not hid. I said, I will confess my transgressions unto the Lord; and thou forgavest the iniquity of my sin.

Psalm 32:1-5

David, as well as the other Old Testament saints, seemed to have had a better understanding of sin, transgression, and iniquity than the body of Christ has today. He probably knew that sexual sin was a weakness or iniquity passed from generation to generation in his family tree. As you follow his descendants, you'll see this iniquity in his sons: Amnon, who raped his half sister, Tamar; and Solomon, who had seven hundred wives and three hundred concubines; and Solomon's son, Rehoboam, who also had many wives and concubines.

When David said, "Blessed is the man whose transgression is forgiven," he was admitting his guilt, repenting to God, and asking for His forgiveness. His confession was part of the pruning of his family tree. We know from reading the Scriptures that David loved God and His Word and received revelation from the Holy Spirit. Even so, he was subject to a family iniquity of sexual sin that eventually led to murder. Although it would have been very easy, he did not give up on himself or his family. He allowed God to prune him.

Had David not confessed, a generational curse of iniquity would have continued in his bloodline and his seed would have had to be destroyed. However, because David confessed and repented, many of his descendants walked in generational blessings instead of the curse.

Once David allowed the pruning process to take place and was cleansed of sexual sin, God's promise of posterity and blessing was inherited by the next generation:

Now the days of David drew nigh that he should die; and he charged Solomon his son, saying...keep

the charge of the Lord thy God, to walk in his ways, to keep his statutes, and his commandments, and his judgments, and his testimonies, as it is written in the law of Moses, that thou mayest prosper in all that thou doest, and whithersoever thou turnest thyself: that the Lord may continue his word which he spake concerning me, saying, If thy children take heed to their way, to walk before me in truth with all their heart and with all their soul, there shall not fail thee (said he) a man on the throne of Israel.

1 Kings 2:1,3,4

Although David committed adultery and had a man murdered, his sins were covered by the blood of sacrifice. God saw David as righteous and blessed his family tree. He said the house of David would never end. And it won't. Jesus came from the seed of David, and we are joint heirs with Him.

THE MATURATION PROCESS

The maturation process of your family tree is guaranteed as long as you continue to feed your family the Word of God and allow the Holy Spirit to water and prune it. Maturity is a process that should take place in every Christian's life. Once you have planted a good family tree, there are some very practical things you and your family should do to aid in your spiritual growth and the godly inheritance of the next generation. These things include being water baptized, regular church attendance, daily prayer and Bible reading, and being baptized in the Holy Spirit.

WATER BAPTISM

Being water baptized is more than being immersed in cold water. Water baptism is a picture or symbol of the old nature of a person and his family iniquities passing away and the new nature of Christ being born in him, thus making him an heir to abundant and eternal life. It is symbolic of Jesus' death, burial and resurrection. I was twenty-three years old when I was water baptized. I had been sprinkled as a baby, but I needed to obey the Scriptures and repent and be baptized:

> **Then they that gladly received his word were baptized.**
>
> **Acts 2:41**

CHURCH ATTENDANCE

One of the ways you and your family will grow spiritually is through regular church attendance. There is a corporate anointing or strength that comes from fellowshiping on a regular basis with other believers, and the Holy Spirit will also water the seed of the Word that you and your family have sown in your hearts during your personal times of devotion. God's Word commands you to become a part of a local body:

> **Not forsaking the assembling of ourselves together; as the manner of some is.**
>
> **Hebrews 10:25**

DAILY PRAYER

Daily prayer is essential to the success of every Christian and Christian family. Prayer is not only a direct line of communication to your heavenly Father, but it is what helps you to "abide in the vine" as you are admonished to do in John 15. Paul exhorts you to "pray without ceasing" (1 Thess. 5:17).

Before she got married, my daughter Sarah met a young man at a secular university she was attending. She said that she liked him and was seeing him on occasion. She also told me he was not saved, and it burdened me. You know how we parents are: we're very watchful of our children.

I don't know why I was so troubled about this young man, but I prayed for him. I didn't think it was good for Sarah to be friendly with him, but try to tell that to a twenty-four year-old! She told me one day, "Well, Mother, he's only a friend." The Lord gave me a Scripture to give to Sarah from James that says not to make friends with the world. (James 4:4.)

The next day I said, "The Lord gave me something I want to share with you." I gave her the Scripture and explained to her that I didn't believe she was even supposed to be friends with this man. Well, she was not happy with me or with God. She sought God in prayer and said, "Why did You tell my mother this; why couldn't You have told me Yourself?"

When she and I were talking about it, I said, "If I told you first, you wouldn't have listened, but if I prayed about it first, I knew God would be able to deal with it." Needless to say, Sarah quit seeing the young man.

Daily prayer for you and your family can bring you to a place of trust and fellowship with God. It also can keep the lines of communication open so that God can speak to you and your family and give you the answers to the challenges you will face in life. A daily prayer life can give you the strength to overcome your family's iniquities and is a must for the maturation process of you and your family tree.

DAILY BIBLE READING

If you want to break the curse and establish the blessings in your family tree, then daily Bible reading is a must in your life. It is the Word that the Holy Spirit will water as you and your family mature in the things of God:

Study to shew thyself approved unto God, a workman that needeth not to be ashamed, rightly dividing the word of truth.

2 Timothy 2:15

If you want to break the curse and establish the blessings in your family tree, then daily Bible reading is a must in your life.

It is very important that Christians feed themselves on the Word of God. People will tell me, "I'm just not fed at my church." My response to them is, "Do you have a Bible?" They respond, "Yes." I'll say, "Can you read?" Their answer of course is, "Yes." Then I will ask, "Then why don't you feed yourself?"

Depending on your church to feed you and your family is not enough. You have to feed on the Word daily yourself. As a matter of fact, you and your family should make it a habit of reading through the Bible every year. If you read two Old Testament chapters and one New Testament chapter six days a week, and three Old Testament and two New Testament chapters on the seventh day of the week, you will have read through the Bible in one year! Reading through the Bible on a daily basis will keep you and your family clean of generational iniquities, encouraged about the things of God, and walking in His promises. Nothing can beat it!

THE BAPTISM OF THE HOLY SPIRIT

When you become born again, you are born of the Spirit. However, to enhance the power of your prayers as well as your understanding of the Word, you and your children and your children's children can be baptized in the Holy Spirit and be filled with the power of God:

> **But ye shall receive power, after that the Holy Ghost is come upon you.**
>
> **Acts 1:8**

> **For the promise is unto you, and to your children, and to all that are afar off, even as many as the Lord our God shall call.**
>
> **Acts 2:39**

The Holy Spirit in your life is your well of living water that Jesus spoke about in John 7:38. He said, "He that believeth in me, as the scripture hath said, out of his belly shall flow rivers of living water." The Holy Spirit wants to be a river of living water to your innermost being. He wants to refresh you spiritually:

> **But whosoever drinketh of the water that I shall give him shall never thirst; but the water that I shall give him shall be in him a well of water springing up to everlasting life.**
>
> **John 4:14**

You are not "less saved" if you aren't baptized in the Holy Spirit; neither are you "more saved" if you are. God wants you to be baptized with the Holy Spirit so that He can empower you spiritually, just as Jesus was empowered spiritually. You were already given the Holy Spirit when you were born again. Now you just have to receive His baptism. By doing so you are receiving His fullness into every area of your life, into every "room" of your being.

It is God's will for you to be born again, water baptized, and filled with the Holy Spirit, but it's up to you! The baptism of the Holy Spirit is God's miracle to bring His character and power into your life so that you can be a bold witness for Him:

> [I pray] **that he would grant you, according to the riches of his glory, to be strengthened with might by his Spirit in the inner man.**
>
> **Ephesians 3:16**

THE FRUIT OF THE SPIRIT

The purpose of a heritage of blessings in your family tree is that you and your descendants benefit from the good fruit or blessings promised by God in His Word. Both individually and as a family, the indwelling of the Holy Spirit enables you to uproot the family iniquities at work in your lives and bear spiritual fruit that will remain:

> **But the fruit of the Spirit is love, joy, peace, longsuffering, gentleness, goodness, faith, meekness, temperance: against such there is no law.**
>
> **Galatians 5:22,23**

All fruit has seed in it. Our fruit of the Spirit leaves seed for the next generation. Praise God that you can pass on good seed and fruit for your family to inherit. Although weeds from the evil tree may still come up from time to time, they will eventually be choked out by your spiritual fruit because the Word of God guarantees that "against such

All fruit has seed in it. Our fruit of the Spirit leaves seed for the next generation.

[the things of the Spirit] there is no law" (Gal. 5:23).

Specific Steps You Can Take
To Grow a Healthy Family Tree

Plant the Seed

The "seed" represents the Word. The "soil" represents your heart.

When planting, make sure you are planting in the most fertile soil. Seed sown along the pathway will not take root and can easily be blown away by temptation. The Word here is planted in the head but not in the heart. Seed sown in rocky soil is joyfully received with superficial understanding. But when life gets tough, the commitment is gone and the seed soon withers and dies. Seed sown in thorny soil is similar to rocky ground. The cares and pleasures of the world will soon choke out the seed until it becomes unfruitful. Good, solid soil can yield one hundred times more than what was sown.

Cultivate

Make a commitment to apply the Word in every area of your life.

Feed and Nurture

Do this through daily devotions, Scripture memorization, and discussing the Word with your family.

Water

Allow the Holy Spirit to give meaning and life to the Word as you apply it in your daily life.

Prune

Cut the dead limbs off and remove dead leaves such as anger, laziness, sickness, and a bad attitude. Remove everything that hinders natural growth.

Mature

Continue solid growth, by following practical spiritual steps:
Water baptism   Regular church attendance   Daily prayer
Bible reading   Baptism in the Holy Spirit

Chart 9

19

HOW TO FACE THE ATTACK
IF THE DEVIL COMES BACK

In the previous chapter, we examined how to begin a heritage of blessings for your family tree. We discovered that depositing the Word of God in your own heart and in the hearts of your family members will provide power to purge the iniquities inherent in your bloodline and set you free to establish a pattern of covenant blessings.

If you'll recall in Matthew 13, Jesus tells the parable of the tares and wheat. He compares them to the types of seed that are planted and cultivated in a person's heart. He said that the seed, which is symbolic of the Word of God, was sown into good ground. But while the husbandman slept, the enemy came and sowed bad seed among the good. Thus, when the sower's seed began to sprout, the bad seed sprouted right alongside of the good:

The kingdom of heaven is likened unto a man which sowed good seed in his field: but while men slept, his enemy came and sowed tares among the wheat, and went his way. But when the blade was sprung up, and brought forth fruit, then appeared the tares also.

Matthew 13:24-26

Good seed and evil seed were planted in the hearts of your forefathers long before you were ever born, and it will take diligence to free your family tree of those weeds of sin. The tares and the wheat, the evil and the good, the curses and the blessings, grow side by side. As a result of Adam and Eve's transgression, you can't have one without the other. Even after you have broken the family curse and established generational blessings, you will still have to contend with the weeds—the sins of your forefathers—that may resurface from time to time. Don't be alarmed, however; through the Word of God and the blood of Jesus, you can combat Satan and win.

WEEDING YOUR FAMILY TREE

I have a friend who pastors in a small town in a fairly large state. He and his wife have four sons and an adopted daughter. When his daughter turned thirteen, she became wild and began to sneak out at night. Her school called and said she was creating problems at school because she was trying to date boys, which her father did not want her to do because she was so young.

After the father pondered the situation, he realized he'd never had that kind of problem with his two older sons. He began to fast and pray for his daughter, asking God what was wrong and what he should do. The Lord spoke to him and said that he was dealing with a family iniquity or generational curse which was coming through the bloodline of his daughter's biological parents.

Living in a small town, he was able to trace her family tree. He knew his daughter's mother and knew that she had given birth out of wedlock to his adopted daughter. He discovered that his daughter's biological mother and grandmother were also illegitimate. He prayed and bound the devil on behalf of his adopted daughter, but God told him that because his daughter was at the age of accountability, she would have to make the choice and bind the devil herself.

This man explained to his daughter that she was illegitimate and that her mother and grandmother were illegitimate also. Then he told her that by the choices she was making, she was establishing a pattern of sin; it was very evident that she was following in her mother's and grandmother's footsteps and would probably get pregnant and have an illegitimate child too.

"This is the devil's set-up for you," he explained to her. "Do you want God's divine destiny for you or the devil's?"

This girl's father and mother had been diligent in training their children to serve the Lord. They had planted the seed of God's Word in this girl's heart, and at the time of her father's conversation with her, the Holy Spirit watered the Word that had been planted. Consequently, God gave her revelation of what her father was saying, and the girl chose to obey her father's instructions.

The girl understood immediately what her father was talking about. An evil spirit familiar with her family's history of sexual sin was trying to influence her to go the way of her forefathers. "Dad," she said, "I don't want to go that route." She repented and was cleansed of her biological family's iniquity. As a result, she was a virgin when she got married and is still serving God today!

STAND AGAINST THE DEVIL

We know how familiar spirits operate: an unclean or familiar spirit will try to reenter a future generation, just like it did with this pastor's daughter. It will stalk your child or grandchild like a rapist stalks his victim. It will watch for the perfect timing—the right age or circumstance—to attack. If you used to smoke, drink, or take drugs, then it will watch for a certain age to tempt your child with the same thing.

> *An unclean or familiar spirit will try to reenter a future generation... It will stalk your child or grandchild like a rapist stalks his victim.*

The good news is you don't have to put up with Satan's tactics! You can stop him in his tracks and let him know that your family tree is off limits because God's covenant of generational blessings has been promised to you and your family and it extends to a thousand generations:

Know therefore that the Lord thy God, he is God, the faithful God, which keepeth covenant and mercy with them that love him and keep his commandments to a thousand generations.

Deuteronomy 7:9

"How," you may ask, "can I stop Satan in his tracks?" By disarming him! If you read of the wars in the Old Testament, you'll find many references to Israel's spoiling their enemies' goods. To spoil means "to plunder" or to take the property of another by force, to strip a person of their power and possessions.

How can one enter into a strong man's house, and spoil his goods, except he first bind the strong man? and then he will spoil his house.

Matthew 12:29

Remember, the strong man referred to in this text is the devil. You can bind him in your family tree just like my pastor friend tried to do for his daughter. But because she was of age, God said she had to bind the devil from operating in her family herself. No one else could do it for her. James 4:7 says, "Submit yourselves therefore to God. Resist the devil, and he will flee from you." Bind the devil in the name of Jesus. Each time you do this, you strip him of his power and his possessions—your family tree.

Regardless of what iniquities are in your background—drugs, sexual perversion, or so forth—do your children a favor and be honest with them. Wait for the right age to warn them about the various things the devil may try to tempt them with and why; tell them it's a generational iniquity. Explain to them that you have repented of your past and have therefore been cleansed by the blood of Jesus. Therefore, you and your future generations are free, although the devil would like to reenter your bloodline through them.

If your children or grandchildren are already following a pattern of generational iniquity, then deal with them openly and honestly, like my pastor friend did. If you fail to do this and that familiar spirit is allowed to continue influencing them, the iniquity will become more and more of a stronghold and will increase in its intensity. What started out as anger in you can develop into uncontrolled violence in your offspring and murder in the next generation. Let's look at our text once again:

> **And when he is come, he findeth it empty, swept, and garnished. Then goeth he, and taketh with himself *seven other spirits more wicked than himself, and they enter in and dwell there: and the last state of that man is worse than the first.***
>
> **Matthew 12:44,45**

Perhaps you're beginning to see some things in your children that, after having read this chapter, are quite alarming. Don't be discouraged, however; the Word is greater than any sins your children may be involved in and any generational iniquity. Keep the Word before you. Quote it to yourself, the devil, and your family. You may say, "I've made mistakes as a parent!" Well, so have a million other parents. I haven't met a perfect parent yet.

God will bring you and your family through to a place of victory and blessing in Him. Do not become alarmed or discouraged by the weeds that may poke through the soil of your loved ones' hearts from time to time. The Word and

> *God will bring you and your family through to a place of victory and blessing in Him.*

the blood of Jesus are working to cleanse your bloodline. Continue speaking and doing what it says, praising God that whom He has blessed cannot be cursed. (Num. 22:12.)

20

WHEN YOU ARE WEAK,
HE IS STRONG

G od is a good God, and the devil is a bad devil. He doesn't give up his territory easily, nor will he take no for an answer. In Luke 4, Satan tempted Jesus in the wilderness. After he failed, the Bible says he departed from Jesus *for a season.* (v. 13.) The devil was foolish enough to believe that through his persistence, he could cause the Son of God to sin.

Satan will try the same tactic with you and your family; he will attempt to wear down and destroy your family tree. I once knew a pastor who loved God and was probably one of the most powerful pastors I have ever known. He was mightily used of God until he became involved in an affair with his secretary. This iniquity was passed to his two sons, who also became involved in sexual sin. Today, this pastor is no longer in the ministry.

What caused this man to fall? We know and understand from previous chapters that this was a family iniquity of sexual sin. This pastor didn't wake up one morning and say, "You know, today I'm going to ruin my life and that of my family's by having an affair with my secretary." No, it didn't happen like that. The familiar spirits that followed his family tree knew there was a family weakness to sexual sin. They watched and waited for just the right time to tempt this pastor and pressure him until he finally succumbed to the weakness he had inherited from his forefathers.

What this pastor did not realize, however, is that the moment he yielded in this area, he sold his sons as slaves on the sexual sin auction block. Had he resisted the temptation, the curse would have been reversed and the demons that tempted him would not have had such an easy inroad into the lives of his two sons. He could have established a family blessing.

My point is that I believe this pastor tried to resist the temptation to sin with his secretary in his own strength. Perhaps he was too embarrassed to share what was happening to him with a trusted friend. Or maybe he thought, *It'll never happen to me. I'm stronger than that!*

Tragically, because he gave in and allowed the sin to remain unconfessed, a door was opened for the devil to come in and wreak havoc in this man's life and the lives of his descendants. If he had repented when the thoughts to commit adultery first occurred, then when the devil came to tempt him, he would have had God's strength to resist him. The devil would have had a hard time tempting him at all because he would not have been able to cross the bloodline of Jesus Christ.

In cleansing your bloodline and beginning a heritage of blessings for your family tree, I want you to know that the power of God is present to help you and you don't have to do it in your own strength. The Bible says that Jesus took your infirmities and bore your sicknesses. A simple definition of the word *infirmity* is an area of your life in which you are not firm. For example, a person may not be firm in the area of finances; he always spends his money foolishly. Someone else may not be firm in the area of diet. That person is overweight and constantly fighting the same battle to lose or maintain a certain weight.

Jesus took your infirmities, so unlike my pastor friend, you don't have to try to resist the devil in your own strength. All you have to do is obey the Word in the area of finances or in the areas that you are "unfirm." For example, Malachi 3 talks about the blessings that come with tithing. If you want to reverse the curse in the area of finances, then begin to tithe and give alms and offerings according to God's Word. By doing this, you are acknowledging that Jesus has paid the price, once and for all, and the areas in which you were unfirm become supernaturally strengthened.

THE FAITH WALK

In the previous chapter, we discovered that the devil will look for an opportunity to afflict you with your forefathers' sins. However, Jesus was bruised for your iniquities, and you don't have to take the devil's bruisings anymore. Jesus' blood has cleansed your family tree, and you are free to produce good, healthy fruit in this and the next generation.

Second Corinthians 5:7 says, "For we walk by faith, not by sight." The Holy Spirit has reminded me of this many times. As a parent, as a pastor's wife, as the founder and president of Marilyn Hickey Ministries, there have been times in my life when I have said to God, "I'm doing what your Word tells me to do, but what am I doing wrong?"

"You must do it by faith, Marilyn," has been God's reply, "not sight."

Faith is simply acting as though the Word of God is true. Faith is thanking God for the answer *before* you receive the outward manifestation. Faith is ceasing from your own efforts to make your prayers work and resting in the promises of His Word that it is already done.

What I've shared with you in the pages of this book you will have to act on by faith. There may be times, for example, after you have followed the steps for cleansing your family tree and beginning a heritage of blessings that things will become progressively worse. From time to time you may even wonder, *How much more can I take?* Don't throw in the towel! It is during these times that I want to assure you that you can rest in God's promises:

> **God is not mocked: for whatsoever** [you] **soweth, that shall** [you] **also reap.**
>
> Galatians 6:7

> **Be not afraid nor dismayed by reason of this great multitude;** *for the battle is not yours, but God's.*
>
> 2 Chronicles 20:15

When You Are Weak, Then You Are Strong

God's Word is His covenant, His contractual agreement with you that He cannot and will not break—He will do what the Bible says He will do. Of all the agreements, contracts, treaties, or pacts ever devised by man, none is more binding upon the parties involved than your covenant with God. It is based on His Son's shed blood and is an exchange of Jesus' strength for your weaknesses.

When you became born again, Jesus took your weaknesses of the flesh in exchange for His supernatural ability and strength. Because of your covenant with Him, you and the members of your family tree are supernaturally empowered to overcome in areas of your life that, up until the time of salvation, you had consistently failed in.

Through His death, Jesus has become your strength. Through His death came resurrection life. Through His shed blood, the very iniquities that have held you and your family bound were rendered powerless:

> **Having canceled the written code, with its regulations, that was against us and that stood opposed to us; he took it away, nailing it to the cross. And having disarmed the powers and authorities, he made a public spectacle of them, triumphing over them by the cross.**
>
> **Colossians 2:14,15** NIV

The apostle Paul understood the significance and purpose of his covenant with God. He realized that living the Christian life had nothing to do with his natural talents or abilities. It was Christ in him who equipped and enabled him to do the supernatural. Paul's weaknesses were a source of joy to him because he knew that where his abilities ended, God's supernatural power began:

> **Therefore I take pleasure in infirmities, in reproaches, in necessities, in persecutions, in distresses for Christ's sake:** *for when I am weak, then am I strong.*
>
> **2 Corinthians 12:10**

Paul said, "I get happy when I'm weak. I get so happy when people talk about me, when I run out of money, when people persecute me and throw rocks at me. I get so happy in distresses, because when I am weak, then am I strong!"

"How," you might ask, "can a person become strong when he's weak?" The answer is simple: God's grace. It was sufficient for Paul, and it is sufficient for you and the members of your family tree. Grace is God's unmerited favor, or His ability to put you over in any situation. It is a gift from God; you don't have to do anything short of becoming saved in order to receive it. Paul had a revelation of God's grace and understood how to rest in it.

In 2 Corinthians 12:9, Paul said he would glory in his infirmities so the power of God could rest upon him. The word *infirmities* is another word for "weaknesses." Had my pastor friend realized that where he was weak in the flesh God's power could supernaturally strengthen him, then he may not have yielded to sexual sin.

How often do you depend on God's grace when you're in the throes of a difficult situation? When was the last time you were overcome with joy when your offspring, for the umpteenth time, yielded to that same family sin? Nehemiah 8:10 says the joy of the Lord is your strength, but I'm almost certain that few in the body of Christ glory in their tribulations or find an abundance of joy and peace during times of trouble.

Although Paul wrote two-thirds of the New Testament and is considered by many as a great man of God, he understood his weakness in the flesh. Because of the abundance of revelations, he said he was given "a thorn in the flesh, the messenger of Satan to buffet me" (2 Cor. 12:7). Paul prayed to God three times to remove this thorn, but God's response was, "You can handle it, Paul. My power is resting upon you, giving you the strength you need in this situation":

My grace is sufficient for thee: for my strength is made perfect in weakness.

2 Corinthians 12:9

The word *perfect* in this passage of Scripture means "to complete, to consummate."[1] God assured Paul that the thorn in his flesh was according to His will, that His grace would be provided to Paul to endure or suffer all things. Paul had to learn to depend wholly upon the power of God so that His strength could be consummated or brought to full term in Paul's life.

You may think, *I'm weak. There's no way I can reverse the curse in my life, much less in my family tree.* But you can. First Corinthians 1:27 says God uses the weak things of this world to confound the mighty! Changing the tide of this and the next generation can only be done through God's grace. It will take His strength and not a man-made formula to weed the garden of your family tree and to separate the tares from the wheat.

Establishing and maintaining a heritage of generational blessings is a supernatural act, not a natural one. It can only be accomplished in the spirit realm because the devil wants to permanently enslave the members of your family. Many Christians think that the devil can be overcome by following a few simple steps, but we know this is not the case. Because of the "mystery of iniquity" referred to in 2 Thessalonians 2:7, God's grace is the only key to overcoming generational iniquities, and you must learn to rely on His power resting upon you and your future generations.

Don't become too upset about your family's weaknesses or predispositions toward certain inherited sin. Imitate the apostle

Paul and glory in them, realizing that it is God's opportunity to perfect His strength in you. As you confess God's grace—His supernatural and perfected strength in your life—you will experience the power of His blood, that divine, supernatural cleansing agent, that Christ shed at Calvary to free you and your future generations from the curse of family iniquities.

Pray this prayer out loud and remind the devil that the blood of Jesus and God's grace are more than sufficient to maintain a heritage of blessings for your family tree:

> *Father, I thank You that Jesus Christ has given us all we need to deliver us from every sin, trespass, and iniquity. The blood is enough. I declare these iniquities* [name each iniquity], *and I repent of them and receive the cleansing of the blood. Thank You that this bruise belongs to Jesus, who was bruised for my iniquities. When the enemy tries to come, he will encounter the blood. I will remind him that this part of my life that was weak is now strong because of God's grace and Jesus' blood and the Spirit bears witness to the blood. The anointing is also there, and the anointing has destroyed that yoke. In Jesus' name, Satan, you are defeated, and you'll never destroy me or my household! Amen.*

Because of the blood of Jesus, you and your family are no longer victims of your past. The devil is defeated, and your best days are yet ahead. You have reversed the tide of family iniquities in your lives and are free to establish generations of blessings. Praise God *now* for victory for you, your children, and *the next generation!*

Appendix

CURSES AND BLESSINGS

In this appendix, I have provided a list of different generational curses which may affect your family. For each curse, I have provided Scripture verses on which you can stand to break the curse in your life and your family's lives.

THE CURSE: GENERAL HEALTH PROBLEMS
THE BLESSING:

He sent his word, and healed them, and delivered them from their destructions. (Psalm 107:20)

Surely he hath borne our griefs, and carried our sorrows.... He was wounded for our transgressions, he was bruised for our iniquities: the chastisement of our

peace was upon him; and with his stripes we are healed.
(Isaiah 53:4,5)

Let the weak say, I am strong. (Joel 3:10)

Beloved, I wish above all things that thou mayest prosper and be in health, even as thy soul prospereth.
(3 John 2)

Who his own self bare our sins in his own body on the tree, that we, being dead to sins, should live unto righteousness: by whose stripes ye were healed.
(1 Peter 2:24)

THE CURSE: ABDOMINAL PAIN
THE BLESSING:

Be not wise in thine own eyes: fear the Lord, and depart from evil. It shall be health to thy navel, and marrow to thy bones. (Proverbs 3:7,8)

THE CURSE: ADULTERY
THE BLESSING:

Marriage is honourable in all, and the bed undefiled: but whoremongers and adulterers God will judge.
(Hebrews 13:4)

Reproofs of instruction are the way of life: to keep thee from the evil woman, from the flattery of the tongue of a strange woman. Lust not after her beauty in thine heart. (Proverbs 6:23-25)

THE CURSE: ALCOHOLISM
THE BLESSING:

O taste and see that the LORD is good: blessed is the man that trusteth in him. (Psalm 34:8)

If any man thirst, let him come unto me, and drink. (John 7:37)

Jesus answered and said unto her, Whosoever drinketh of this water shall thirst again: but whosoever drinketh of the water that I shall give him will never thirst; but the water that I shall give him shall be in him a well of water springing up into everlasting life. (John 4:13,14) Shivambu

Then they cried unto the LORD in their trouble, and he delivered them out of their distresses. (Psalm 107:6)

And it shall come to pass, that whosoever shall call on the name of the Lord shall be delivered. (Joel 2:32)

If the Son therefore shall make you free, ye shall be free indeed. (John 8:36)

For the law of the Spirit of life in Christ Jesus hath made me free from the law of sin and death. (Romans 8:2)

THE CURSE: ARTHRITIS
THE BLESSING:

Behold, thou hast instructed many, and thou hast strengthened the weak hands. Thy words have upholden him that was falling, and thou hast strengthened the feeble knees. (Job 4:3,4)

Wherefore lift up the hands which hang down, and the feeble knees; and make straight paths for your feet, lest that which is lame be turned out of the way; but let it rather be healed. (Hebrews 12:12,13)

THE CURSE: ASTHMA AND COLDS
THE BLESSING:

Why art thou cast down, O my soul? and why art thou disquieted within me? hope thou in God: for I shall yet praise him, who is the health of my countenance, and my God. (Psalm 42:11)

Seeing he giveth to all life, and breath, and all things. (Acts 17:25)

THE CURSE: ARGUMENTATIVE NATURE
THE BLESSING:

How forcible are right words! but what doth your arguing reprove? (Job 6:25)

THE CURSE: BACK PAIN
THE BLESSING:

The Lord upholdeth all that fall, and raiseth up all those that be bowed down. (Psalm 145:14)

THE CURSE: BACKSLIDING
THE BLESSING:

These things have I written unto you that believe on the name of the Son of God; that ye may know that ye have eternal life. (1 John 5:13)

I know whom I have believed, and am persuaded that he is able to keep that which I have committed unto him against that day. (2 Timothy 1:12)

Hereby know we that we dwell in him, and he in us, because he hath given us of his Spirit. (1 John 4:13)

The Spirit itself beareth witness with our spirit, that we are the children of God. (Romans 8:16)

THE CURSE: BLOOD DISEASE
(LEUKEMIA, ABNORMAL BLOOD PRESSURE, DIABETES)
THE BLESSING:

I said unto thee when thou wast in thy blood, Live; yea, I said unto thee when thou wast in thy blood, Live. (Ezekiel 16:6)

Behold, I will bring it health and cure, and I will cure them, and will reveal unto them the abundance of peace and truth. (Jeremiah 33:6)

Confess your faults one to another; and pray one for another, that ye may be healed. The effectual fervent prayer of a righteous man availeth much. (James 5:16)

For I will cleanse their blood that I have not cleansed. (Joel 3:21)

THE CURSE: BONE DISEASE
THE BLESSING:

Pleasant words are as an honeycomb, sweet to the soul, and health to the bones. (Proverbs 16:24)

Have mercy upon me, O Lord; for I am weak: O Lord, heal me; for my bones are vexed. (Psalm 6:2)

THE CURSE: BROKEN BONES
THE BLESSING:

He keepeth all his bones: not one of them is broken. (Psalm 34:20)

THE CURSE: BURNS
THE BLESSING:

When thou walkest through the fire, thou shalt not be burned; neither shall the flame kindle upon thee. (Isaiah 43:2)

The Lord is thy shade upon thy right hand. The sun shall not smite thee by day, nor the moon by night. (Psalm 121:5,6)

THE CURSE: CANCER
THE BLESSING:

For verily I say unto you, That whosoever shall say unto this mountain, Be thou removed, and be thou cast into the sea; and shall not doubt in his heart, but shall believe that those things which he saith shall come to pass; he shall have whatsoever he saith. Therefore I say unto you, What things soever ye desire, when ye pray, believe that ye receive them, and ye shall have them. (Mark 11:23,24)

Every plant, which my heavenly Father hath not planted, shall be rooted up. (Matthew 15:13)

THE CURSE: CONDEMNATION
THE BLESSING:

There is therefore now no condemnation to them which are in Christ Jesus. (Romans 8:1)

THE CURSE: DEMONIC ATTACK
THE BLESSING:

Wherefore take unto you the whole armour of God, that ye may be able to withstand in the evil day, and having done all, to stand. Stand therefore, having your loins girt about with truth, and having on the breastplate of righteousness; and your feet shod with the preparation of the gospel of peace; above all, taking the shield of faith, wherewith ye shall be able to quench all the fiery darts of the wicked. And take the helmet of salvation, and the sword of the Spirit, which is the word of God: praying always with all prayer and supplication in the Spirit. (Ephesians 6:13-18)

THE CURSE: DISHONESTY
THE BLESSING:

Providing for honest things, not only in the sight of the Lord, but also in the sight of men. (2 Corinthians 8:21)

Neither give place to the devil. (Ephesians 4:27)

Recompense to no man evil for evil. Provide things honest in the sight of all men. (Romans 12:17)

Create in me a clean heart, O God; and renew a right spirit within me. (Psalm 51:10)

THE CURSE: EYE AND EAR PROBLEMS
THE BLESSING:

The Lord openeth the eyes of the blind. (Psalm 146:8)

And the eyes of them that see shall not be dim, and the ears of them that hear shall hearken. (Isaiah 32:3)

And in that day shall the deaf hear the words of the book, and the eyes of the blind shall see out of obscurity, and out of darkness. (Isaiah 29:18)

Then the eyes of the blind shall be opened, and the ears of the deaf shall be unstopped. (Isaiah 35:5)

The blind receive their sight...and the deaf hear. (Matthew 11:5)

THE CURSE: FATIGUE, INFIRMITY, WEAKNESS
THE BLESSING:

He giveth power to the faint; and to them that have no might he increaseth strength.... But they that wait upon the Lord shall renew their strength. (Isaiah 40:29,31)

Though I walk in the midst of trouble, thou wilt revive me: thou shalt stretch forth thine hand...and thy right hand shall save me. (Psalm 138:7)

But the spirit giveth life. (2 Corinthians 3:6)

THE CURSE: FEARFULNESS, SHYNESS
THE BLESSING:

I can do all things through Christ which strengtheneth me. (Philippians 4:13)

Greater is he that is in you, than he that is in the world. (1 John 4:4)

But ye shall receive power, after that the Holy Ghost is come upon you: and ye shall be witnesses unto me. (Acts 1:8)

The wicked flee when no man pursueth: but the righteous are bold as a lion. (Proverbs 28:1)

The people that do know their God shall be strong, and do exploits. (Daniel 11:32)

THE CURSE: FEAR OF MAN
THE BLESSING:

Nay, in all these things we are more than conquerors through him that loved us. (Romans 8:37)

In God I will praise his word, in God I have put my trust; I will not fear what flesh can do unto me. (Psalm 56:4)

THE CURSE: FEAR OF OLD AGE
THE BLESSING:

Bless the Lord, O my soul: and all that is within me, bless his holy name. Bless the Lord, O my soul, and forget not all his benefits: who forgiveth all thine iniquities; who healeth all thy diseases; who redeemeth thy life from destruction; who crowneth thee with lovingkindness and tender mercies; who satisfieth thy mouth with good things; so that thy youth is renewed like the eagle's. (Psalm 103:1-5)

The righteous...shall still bring forth fruit in old age; they shall be fat and flourishing. (Psalm 92:12,14)

THE CURSE: FOOT TROUBLE
THE BLESSING:

For thou hast delivered my soul from death, mine eyes from tears, and my feet from falling. I will walk before the Lord in the land of the living. (Psalm 116:8,9)

Then shalt thou walk in thy way safely, and thy foot shall not stumble. (Proverbs 3:23)

THE CURSE: FOOLISH SPEECH
THE BLESSING:

Whoso keepeth his mouth and his tongue keepeth his soul from troubles. (Proverbs 21:23)

For he that will love life, and see good days, let him refrain his tongue from evil, and his lips that they speak no guile. (1 Peter 3:10)

He that hath knowledge spareth his words. (Proverbs 17:27)

In the multitude of words there wanteth not sin, but he that refraineth his lips is wise. (Proverbs 10:19)

A man hath joy by the answer of his mouth: and a word spoken in due season, how good is it! (Proverbs 15:23)

Let no corrupt communication proceed out of your mouth, but that which is good to the use of edifying, that it may minister grace unto the hearers. (Ephesians 4:29)

Let your speech be alway with grace, seasoned with salt, that ye may know how ye ought to answer every man. (Colossians 4:6)

Set a watch, O Lord, before my mouth; keep the door of my lips. (Psalm 141:3)

THE CURSE: FOOLISHNESS
THE BLESSING:

But of him are ye in Christ Jesus, who of God is made unto us wisdom. (1 Corinthians 1:30)

THE CURSE: HAND PROBLEMS
THE BLESSING:

Strengthen ye the weak hands, and confirm the feeble knees. (Isaiah 35:3)

THE CURSE: HATEFULNESS
THE BLESSING:

Love one another; as I have loved you, that ye also love one another. (John 13:34)

The love of God is shed abroad in our hearts by the Holy Ghost. (Romans 5:5)

THE CURSE: HEADACHES AND MIGRAINES
THE BLESSING:

But if the Spirit of him that raised up Jesus from the dead dwell in you, he that raised up Christ from the dead shall also quicken your mortal bodies by his Spirit that dwelleth in you. (Romans 8:11)

This is my comfort in my affliction: for thy word hath quickened me. (Psalm 119:50)

THE CURSE: HEART DISEASE
THE BLESSING:

Wait on the LORD: be of good courage, and he shall strengthen thine heart: wait, I say, on the Lord. (Psalm 27:14)

The Lord is my strength and my shield; my heart trusted in him, and I am helped: therefore my heart greatly rejoiceth; and with my song will I praise him. (Psalm 28:7)

Be of good courage, and he shall strengthen your heart, all ye that hope in the Lord. (Psalm 31:24)

Keep thy heart with all diligence; for out of it are the issues of life. (Proverbs 4:23)

A merry heart doeth good like a medicine: but a broken spirit drieth the bones. (Proverbs 17:22)

THE CURSE: INFERIORITY COMPLEX
THE BLESSING:

Yet not I, but Christ liveth in me. (Galatians 2:20)

I know whom I have believed, and am persuaded that he is able to keep that which I have committed unto him. (2 Timothy 1:12)

If God be for us, who can be against us? (Romans 8:31)

So that we may boldly say, The Lord is my helper, and I will not fear what man shall do unto me. (Hebrews 13:6)

Not that we are sufficient of ourselves to think any thing as of ourselves; but our sufficiency is of God. (2 Corinthians 3:5)

Whoso offereth praise glorifieth me. (Psalm 50:23)

For know also, that in the last days perilous times shall come. For men shall be lovers of their ownselves, covetous, boasters, proud, blasphemers, disobedient to parents, unthankful, unholy. (2 Timothy 3:1,2)

Giving thanks always for all things unto God and the Father in the name of our Lord Jesus Christ. (Ephesians 5:20)

By him therefore let us offer the sacrifice of praise to God continually. (Hebrews 13:15)

In every thing give thanks: for this is the will of God in Christ Jesus concerning you. (1 Thessalonians 5:18)

As ye have therefore received Christ Jesus the Lord, so walk ye in him: rooted and built up in him, and established in the faith, as ye have been taught, abounding therein with thanksgiving. (Colossians 2:6,7)

THE CURSE: INFERTILITY
THE BLESSING:

There shall not be male or female barren among you. (Deuteronomy 7:14)

He maketh the barren woman to keep house, and to be a joyful mother of children. (Psalm 113:9)

THE CURSE: INSOMNIA
THE BLESSING:

I will both lay me down in peace, and sleep: for thou, Lord, only makest me dwell in safety. (Psalm 4:8)

It is vain for you to rise up early, to sit up late, to eat the bread of sorrows: for so he giveth his beloved sleep. (Psalm 127:2)

For the Lord hath poured out upon you the spirit of deep sleep, and hath closed your eyes. (Isaiah 29:10)

When thou liest down, thou shalt not be afraid: yea, thou shalt lie down, and thy sleep shall be sweet. (Proverbs 3:24)

THE CURSE: LACK OF FAITH
THE BLESSING:

God hath dealt to every man the measure of faith. (Romans 12:3)

THE CURSE: MENTAL DISORDER
THE BLESSING:

In the multitude of my thoughts within me thy comforts delight my soul. (Psalm 94:19)

The Lord also will be a refuge for the oppressed, a refuge in times of trouble. (Psalm 9:9)

Commit thy works unto the Lord, and thy thoughts shall be established. (Proverbs 16:3)

But we have the mind of Christ. (1 Corinthians 2:16)

Casting down imaginations, and every high thing that exalteth itself against the knowledge of God, and bringing into captivity every thought to the obedience of Christ. (2 Corinthians 10:5)

And the peace of God, which passeth all understanding, shall keep your hearts and minds through Christ Jesus. (Philippians 4:7)

For God hath not given us the spirit of fear; but of power; and of love, and of a sound mind. (2 Timothy 1:7)

THE CURSE: MOUTH, LIP, TONGUE PROBLEMS
THE BLESSING:

Whoso keepeth his mouth and his tongue keepeth his soul from troubles. (Proverbs 21:23)

And straightway his ears were opened, and the string of his tongue was loosed, and he spake plain. And were beyond measure astonished, saying, He hath done all things well: he maketh both the deaf to hear; and the dumb to speak. (Mark 7:35,37)

The mouth of a righteous man is a well of life. (Proverbs 10:11)

He that keepeth his mouth keepeth his life: but he that openeth wide his lips shall have destruction. (Proverbs 13:3)

THE CURSE: MUSCULAR DYSTROPHY
AND MULTIPLE SCLEROSIS
THE BLESSING:

There shall no evil befall thee, neither shall any plague come nigh thy dwelling. For he shall give his angels charge over thee, to keep thee in all thy ways. They shall bear thee up in their hands, lest thou dash thy foot against a stone. (Psalm 91:10-12)

THE CURSE: NEGATIVE SELF-IMAGE
THE BLESSING:

Do ye look on things after the outward appearance? If any man trust to himself that he is Christ's, let him of himself think this again, that, as he is Christ's, even so are we Christ's! (2 Corinthians 10:7)

Herein is our love made perfect, that we may have boldness in the day of judgment: because as he is, so are we in this world (1 John 4:17)

THE CURSE: NERVOUS CONDITION
THE BLESSING:

God is our refuge and strength, a very present help in trouble. (Psalm 46:1)

Cast thy burden upon the Lord, and he shall sustain thee: he shall never suffer the righteous to be moved. (Psalm 55:22)

Where the Spirit of the Lord is, there is liberty. (2 Corinthians 3:17)

THE CURSE: OCCULT PRACTICES
THE BLESSING:

Wherefore God also hath highly exalted him, and given him a name which is above every name: that at the name of Jesus every knee should bow, of things in heaven, and things in earth and things under the earth: and that every tongue should confess that Jesus Christ is Lord, to the glory of God the Father. (Philippians 2:9-11)

Submit yourselves therefore to God. Resist the devil and he will flee from you. (James 4:7)

BREAKING GENERATIONAL CURSES

Lest Satan should get an advantage of us: for we are not ignorant of his devices. (2 Corinthians 2:11)

Behold, I give you power to tread on serpents and scorpions, and over all the power of the enemy: and nothing shall by any means hurt you. (Luke 10:19)

When the enemy shall come in like a flood, the Spirit of the Lord shall lift up a standard against him. (Isaiah 59:19)

And ought not this woman, being a daughter of Abraham, whom Satan hath bound, lo, these eighteen years, be loosed from this bond on the sabbath day? (Luke 13:16)

Put on the whole armour of God, that ye may be able to stand against the wiles of the devil. For we wrestle not against flesh and blood, but against principalities, against powers, against the rulers of the darkness of this world, against spiritual wickedness in high places. (Ephesians 6:11,12)

THE CURSE: OPPRESSION
THE BLESSING:

The Lord is the strength of my life; of whom shall I be afraid? (Psalm 27:1)

If the Son therefore shall make you free, ye shall be free indeed. (John 8:36)

THE CURSE: PALSY AND STROKE
THE BLESSING:

Thy vows are upon me, O God: I will render praises unto thee. For thou hast delivered my soul from death: wilt not thou deliver my feet from falling, that I may walk before God in the light of the living? (Psalm 56:12,13)

THE CURSE: POISONING
THE BLESSING:

They shall take up serpents; and if they drink any deadly thing, it shall not hurt them. (Mark 16:18)

Thou hast clothed me with skin and flesh, and hast fenced me with bones and sinews. Thou hast granted me life and favour, and thy visitation hath preserved my spirit. (Job 10:11)

THE CURSE: POVERTY
THE BLESSING:

But my God shall supply all your need according to his riches in glory by Christ Jesus. (Philippians 4:19)

This book of the law shall not depart out of thy mouth; but thou shalt meditate therein day and night, that thou mayest observe to do according to all that is written therein: for then thou shalt make thy way prosperous, and then thou shalt have good success. (Joshua 1:8)

Blessed is the man that walketh not in the counsel of the ungodly, nor standeth in the way of sinners, nor sitteth in the seat of the scornful. But his delight is in the law of the Lord; and in his law doth he meditate day and night. And he shall be like a tree planted by the rivers of water, that bringeth forth his fruit in his season; his leaf also shall not wither; and whatsoever he doeth shall prosper. (Psalm 1:1-3)

But seek ye first the kingdom of God, and his righteousness; and all these things shall be added unto you. (Matthew 6:33)

But thou shalt remember the Lord thy God: for it is he that giveth thee power to get wealth. (Deuteronomy 8:18)

Beloved, I wish above all things that thou mayest prosper and be in health, even as thy soul prospereth. (3 John 2)

The thief cometh not, but for to steal, and to kill, and to destroy: I am come that they might have life and that they might have it more abundantly. (John 10:10)

Honour the Lord with thy substance, and with the firstfruits of all thine increase: so shall thy barns be filled with plenty, and thy presses shall burst out with new wine. (Proverbs 3:9,10)

Give, and it shall be given unto you; good measure, pressed down, and shaken together, and running over, shall men give into your bosom. For with the same measure that ye mete withal it shall be measured to you again. (Luke 6:38)

*Beloved, if our hearts condemn us not, then have
we confidence toward God. And whatsoever we ask, we
receive of him, because we keep his commandments,
and do those things that are pleasing in his sight.*
(1 John 3:21,22)

THE CURSE: PROFANITY
THE BLESSING:

*But now ye also put off all these; anger, wrath,
malice, blasphemy, filthy communication out of your
mouth.* (Colossians 3:8)

*Pleasant words are as an honeycomb, sweet to the
soul, and health to the bones.* (Proverbs 16:24)

*Death and life are in the power of the tongue: and they
that love it shall eat the fruit thereof.* (Proverbs 18:21)

A wholesome tongue is a tree of life. (Proverbs 15:4)

THE CURSE: REBELLIOUS CHILDREN
THE BLESSING:

*My son, attend to my words; incline thine ear unto
my sayings. Let them not depart from thine eyes; keep
them in the midst of thine heart. For they are life unto
those that find them, and health to all their flesh.*
(Proverbs 4:20-22)

*Thus saith the Lord; Refrain thy voice from
weeping, and thine eyes from tears: for thy work shall
be rewarded, saith the Lord; and they shall come again
from the land of the enemy.* (Jeremiah 31:16)

THE CURSE: SADNESS AND SORROW
THE BLESSING:

Thou wilt shew me the path of life: in thy presence is fulness of joy; at thy right hand there are pleasures for evermore. (Psalm 16:11)

Then he said unto them, Go your way, eat the fat, and drink the sweet, and send portions unto them for whom nothing is prepared: for this day is holy unto our Lord: neither be ye sorry; for the joy of the Lord is your strength. (Nehemiah 8:10)

And ye now therefore have sorrow: but I will see you again, and your hearts shall rejoice, and your joy no man taketh from you. (John 16:22)

Whom having not seen, ye love; in whom, though now ye see him not, yet believing, ye rejoice with joy unspeakable and full of glory. (1 Peter 1:8)

But none of these things move me, neither count I my life dear unto myself, so that I might finish my course with joy. (Acts 20:24)

THE CURSE: SELFISHNESS AND GREED
THE BLESSING:

For God so loved the world, that he gave his only begotten Son, that whosoever believeth in him should not perish, but have everlasting life. (John 3:16)

It is more blessed to give than to receive. (Acts 20:35)

Will a man rob God? Yet ye have robbed me. But ye say, Wherein have we robbed thee? In tithes and offerings. Ye are cursed with a curse: for ye have robbed me, even this whole nation. Bring ye all the tithes into the storehouse, that there may be meat in mine house, and prove me now herewith, saith the Lord of hosts, if I will not open you the windows of heaven, and pour you out a blessing, that there shall not be room enough to receive it. And I will rebuke the devourer for your sakes, and he shall not destroy the fruits of your ground; neither shall your vine cast her fruit before the time in the field, saith the Lord of hosts. And all nations shall call you blessed: for ye shall be a delightsome land, saith the Lord of hosts. (Malachi 3:8-12)

There is that scattereth, and yet increaseth; and there is that withholdeth more than is meet, but it tendeth to poverty. (Proverbs 11:24)

But this I say, He which soweth sparingly shall reap also sparingly; and he which soweth bountifully shall reap also bountifully. Every man according as he purposeth in his heart, so let him give; not grudgingly, or of necessity: for God loveth a cheerful giver. (2 Corinthians 9:6,7)

THE CURSE: SELF-CONSCIOUSNESS
THE BLESSING:

The fear of man bringeth a snare: but whoso putteth his trust in the Lord shall be safe. (Proverbs 29:25)

THE CURSE: SMOKING
THE BLESSING:

He hath delivered my soul in peace from the battle that was against me. (Psalm 55:18)

For I the Lord thy God will hold thy right hand, saying unto thee, Fear not; I will help thee. (Isaiah 41:13)

Know ye not that ye are the temple of God, and that the Spirit of God dwelleth in you? If any man defile the temple of God, him shall God destroy; for the temple of God is holy, which temple ye are. (1 Corinthians 3:16,17)

Thou shalt come to thy grave in a full age like as a shock of corn cometh in his season. (Job 5:26)

For this purpose the Son of God was manifested, that he might destroy the works of the devil. (1 John 3:8)

THE CURSE: SORROW
THE BLESSING:

This is the day which the Lord hath made; we will rejoice and be glad in it. (Psalm 118:24)

Make a joyful noise unto the Lord, all ye lands. Serve the Lord with gladness: come before his presence with singing. Know ye that the Lord he is God: it is he that hath made us, and not we ourselves; we are his people, and the sheep of his pasture. Enter into his gates with thanksgiving, and into his courts with praise: be thankful unto him, and bless his name. For the Lord is good; his mercy is everlasting; and his truth endureth to all generations. (Psalm 100:1-5)

A merry heart maketh a cheerful countenance: but by sorrow of the heart the spirit is broken. (Proverbs 15:13)

Fear thou not; for I am with thee: be not dismayed, for I am thy God: I will strengthen thee; yea, I will help thee; yea, I will uphold thee with the right hand of my righteousness. (Isaiah 41:10)

THE CURSE: ULCERS
THE BLESSING:

He healeth the broken in heart, and bindeth up their wounds. (Psalm 147:3)

THE CURSE: UNFORGIVENESS, BITTERNESS
THE BLESSING:

And when ye stand praying, forgive, if ye have ought against any: that your Father also which is in heaven may forgive you your trespasses. But if ye do not forgive, neither will your Father which is in heaven forgive your trespasses. (Mark 11:25,26)

But I say unto you, Love your enemies, bless them that curse you, do good to them that hate you, and pray for them which despitefully use you, and persecute you; That ye may be the children of your Father which is in heaven: for he maketh his sun to rise on the evil and on the good, and sendeth rain on the just and on the unjust. (Matthew 5:44,45)

THE CURSE: UNSAVED FAMILY
THE BLESSING:

And they said, Believe on the Lord Jesus Christ, and thou shalt be saved, and thy house. (Acts 16:31)

Then Peter said unto them, Repent, and be baptized every one of you in the name of Jesus Christ for the remission of sins, and ye shall receive the gift of the Holy Ghost. For the promise is unto you, and to your children, and to all that are afar off, even as many as the Lord our God shall call. (Acts 2:38,39)

Rejoice, because your names are written in heaven. (Luke 10:20)

For whosoever shall call upon the name of the Lord shall be saved. (Romans 10:13)

THE CURSE: UNSAVED LOVED ONES
THE BLESSING:

That if thou shalt confess with thy mouth the Lord Jesus, and shalt believe in thine heart that God hath raised him from the dead, thou shalt be saved. For with the heart man believeth unto righteousness; and with the mouth confession is made unto salvation. (Romans 10:9,10)

THE CURSE: UNTIMELY DEATH
THE BLESSING:

Ye shall walk in all the ways which the Lord your God hath commanded you, that ye may live, and that it may be well with you, and that ye may prolong your days in the land which ye shall possess. (Deuteronomy 5:33)

THE CURSE: UNWORTHINESS
THE BLESSING:

For he hath made him to be sin for us, who knew no sin; that we might be made the righteousness of God in him (2 Corinthians 5:21)

THE CURSE: WOUNDS
THE BLESSING:

For I will restore health unto thee, and I will heal thee of thy wounds, saith the Lord. (Jeremiah 30:17)

THE CURSE: WORRIES, FRUSTRATION
THE BLESSING:

Delight thyself also in the Lord; and he shall give thee the desires of thine heart. (Psalm 37:4)

Casting all your care upon him; for he careth for you. (1 Peter 5:7)

Rejoice in the Lord alway: and again I say, Rejoice. (Philippians 4:4)

Not that I speak in respect of want: for I have learned, in whatsoever state I am, therewith to be content. (Philippians 4:11)

Be careful for nothing; but in every thing by prayer and supplication with thanksgiving let your requests be made known unto God. And the peace of God, which passeth all understanding, shall keep your hearts and minds through Christ Jesus. (Philippians 4:6,7)

INDEX TO DIAGRAMS

ENDNOTES

Introduction

1 A. E. Winship.

2 Ibid.

Chapter 6

1 Strong, "Hebrew," entry #8035.

Chapter 7

[1]*The American Heritage Dictionary,* s.v. "heredity."

Chapter 11

1 Strong, "Hebrew," entry #3722.

Chapter 14

1 Strong, "Hebrew," entry #6942.

Chapter 18

1 *The American Heritage Dictionary,* s.v. "nurture."

Chapter 20

1 Strong, "Greek," entry #5048.

REFERENCES

A. E. Winship, Abridgement of *Jukes-Edwards*, R. L. Myers & Co., 1900.

The American Heritage Dictionary, 2nd College Ed. Boston: Houghton Mifflin, 1992.

Strong, James. *Strong's Exhaustive Concordance of the Bible* "Hebrews and Chaldee Dictionary," "Greek Dictionary of the New Testament." Nashville: Abingdon, 1890.

PRAYER OF SALVATION

God loves you—no matter who you are, no matter what your past. God loves you so much that He gave His one and only begotten Son for you. The Bible tells us that "…whoever believes in him shall not perish but have eternal life" (John 3:16 NIV). Jesus laid down His life and rose again so that we could spend eternity with Him in heaven and experience His absolute best on earth. If you would like to receive Jesus into your life, say the following prayer out loud and mean it from your heart.

Heavenly Father, I come to You admitting that I am a sinner. Right now, I choose to turn away from sin, and I ask You to cleanse me of all unrighteousness. I believe that Your Son, Jesus, died on the cross to take away my sins. I also believe that He rose again from the dead so that I might be forgiven of my sins and made righteous through faith in Him. I call upon the name of Jesus Christ to be the Savior and Lord of my life. Jesus, I choose to follow You and ask that You fill me with the power of the Holy Spirit. I declare that right now I am a child of God. I am free from sin and full of the righteousness of God. I am saved in Jesus' name. Amen.

If you prayed this prayer to receive Jesus Christ as your Savior for the first time, please contact us on the web at **www.harrisonhouse.com** to receive a free book.

Or you may write to us at

Harrison House
P.O. Box 35035
Tulsa, Oklahoma 74153

ABOUT THE AUTHOR

Marilyn Hickey is no stranger to impacting the lives of millions worldwide. As founder and president of *Marilyn Hickey Ministries,* Marilyn is being used by God to help "cover the earth with the Word." Her mission has been effectively accomplished through various avenues of ministry, such as partnering with other ministries to ship thousands of Bibles into Communist countries; holding crusades in places like Ethiopia, the Philippines, Korea, Haiti, Brazil, Malaysia, Japan, and Honduras and reaching individuals worldwide through television broadcasts seen on networks such as *Black Entertainment Network (BET)* and *Trinity Broadcasting Network (TBN).* In addition, *Marilyn Hickey Ministries* has established a fully accredited two-year Bible college to raise up Christian leaders to carry out God's mission. Marilyn also serves the body of Christ as the chairman of the board of regents for Oral Roberts University and is the only woman serving on the board of directors for Dr. David Yonggi Cho (pastor of the world's largest congregation, Yoido Full Gospel Church).

In addition to her ministry, Marilyn is also a busy wife and mother of two grown children. She is married to Wallace Hickey, pastor of Orchard Road Christian Center in Greenwood Village, Colorado.

OTHER BOOKS BY MARILYN HICKEY

A Cry for Miracles

Angels All Around

Break the Generational Curse

Break the Generational Curse II

Devils, Demons and Deliverance

God's Covenant for Your Family

How To Be a Mature Christian

Know Your Ministry

Maximize Your Day

Names of God

Release the Power of the Blood Covenant

Satan-Proof Your Home

Signs in the Heavens

When Only a Miracle Will Do

Your Total Health Handbook: Spirit, Soul and Body

Beat Tension

Bold Men Win

Born-Again and Spirit-Filled

Bull-Dog Faith

Change Your Life

Children Who Hit the Mark

Conquering Setbacks

Dare To Be an Achiever

Don't Park Here

Experience Long Life

Fasting and Prayer

God's Benefit: Healing

Hold on to Your Dream

How To Win Friends

Keys To Healing Rejection

More Than a Conqueror

Power of Forgiveness

Power of the Blood

Receiving Resurrection Power

Renew Your Mind

Seven Keys To Make You Rich

Solving Life's Problems

Speak the Word

Stand in the Gap

Story of Esther

Tithes, Offerings, Alms: God's Plan for Blessing You!

Winning Over Weight

Women of the Word

To contact Marilyn Hickey,
write:

Marilyn Hickey Ministries
P.O. Box 17340
Denver, Colorado 80217

*Please include your prayer requests
and comments when you write.*

THE HARRISON HOUSE VISION

Proclaiming the truth and the power

Of the Gospel of Jesus Christ

With excellence;

Encouraging Christians to

Live victoriously,

Grow spiritually,

Know God intimately.